D1571621

MAGGIE
AUSTIN
CAKE

Austin, Maggie,
Maggie Austin cake :
artistry and technique /
2017.
33305237934082
sa   04/11/17

MAGGIE AUSTIN CAKE

Artistry AND Technique

MAGGIE AUSTIN

PHOTOGRAPHY BY KATE HEADLEY

HOUGHTON MIFFLIN HARCOURT

BOSTON NEW YORK 2017

Copyright © 2017 by Maggie Austin

Photography © 2017 by Kate Headley

Still Life with Flowers and Fruit by Jan van Huysum, page 21,
and *The Japanese Footbridge* by Claude Monet, page 22, courtesy of the
National Gallery of Art, Washington

All rights reserved

For information about permission to reproduce selections
from this book, write to trade.permissions@hmhco.com or to Permissions,
Houghton Mifflin Harcourt Publishing Company, 3 Park Avenue,
19th Floor, New York, New York 10016.

www.hmhco.com

Library of Congress Cataloging-in-
Publication Data is available.

ISBN 978-0-544-76535-1 (hardcover)
978-0-544-77032-4 (ebook)

Book design and hand-lettering by Laura Palese

Printed in China

TOP 10 9 8 7 6 5 4 3 2 1

For
DAD

CONTENTS

ACKNOWLEDGMENTS

Thank You

My agent, Berta Treitl, for your patient encouragement and sensitive perseverance. That first cup of tea has taken us a long way and I can't wait to see where we go next! My publisher, Houghton Mifflin Harcourt, for sharing my vision and making it happen. My editor, Stephanie Fletcher, for your light touch and keen eye. From the moment we met, I felt so fortunate to have found my ideal match. Book designer Laura Palese, for crafting a beautiful home for all of this work.

Photographer Kate Headley, for your boundless energy and sense of adventure. You were our undaunted partner and I am so proud of what we made together. Stylist Lauren O'Neill, for your extraordinary attention to detail. Jane Covington Restoration, for opening the doors of Old Chapel Farm so graciously, and my friend Nicole Watson, for making the introduction. Something Vintage, for lending us your gorgeous table settings.

My instructors at the French Pastry School, whose passion for the craft ignited my own. My fellow cake designers and sugar artists, past, present, and future. I am so honored to be part of this nurturing and creative community.

My fans and followers, for your overwhelming support and enthusiasm. My students and interns, for sharing your talent and your spirit. My clients, for the absolute pleasure of celebrating with you.

My business partner and sister, Jess, who has always been and will always be at my side.

Finally, my heart goes out to my mom, my dear friends Joli and Diana, my wonderful family, and the loves of my life, my husband, Robert, and our dog, Bessie. Your unconditional support means the world to me. I love you all.

INTRODUCTION

MY JOURNEY TO CAKE design began in the ballet studio. I was four years old the summer my mom signed me up for class. Ballet struck a chord within me; I was drawn to the quiet, repetitive work and attention to detail. For as long as I could remember, becoming a professional dancer was not my dream—it was simply my path.

My ballet career began right out of high school. The work was exhausting but unbelievably rewarding. Every morning, I arrived at the studio energized and excited. Now that I was dancing for an internationally renowned ballet company, the bar was higher but the ritual was the same: training every day to achieve the subtle tilt of the head, the rounded shape of the arm, the clean line of a perfect arabesque.

Suddenly, an injury changed everything. The doctors said I had irreparable damage to a tiny bone in my foot. As a ballet dancer, this meant the inability to go *en pointe*. My dancing career was over.

Ballet had been my focus for twenty years. Without it, I was adrift.

I found solace in the kitchen. As a child, I was always my dad's sous chef, and the ritual of baking, with its precise steps and centuries-old techniques, reminded me of dance. It helped me regain a sense of order in my life. I enrolled in L'Art de la Pâtisserie program at the French Pastry School in Chicago and studied with acclaimed pastry chefs Sébastien Canonne and Jacquy Pfeiffer. When we studied sugar flowers, I was hooked. Like ballet, the crafting of roses, peonies, and other flowers out of sugar required patience and attention to detail, and the results could be astonishingly beautiful. At last I'd found a new discipline through which I could achieve the beauty and artistic expression I craved.

I pursued my new craft with all the intensity I'd brought to ballet. After graduating, I interned at the legendary Charlie Trotter's in Chicago, where I worked with chef Della Gossett preparing elaborate plated desserts. The high pressure and grueling hours were unforgiving. On rare days off, I recovered by working quietly with my sugar flowers. But the frenetic energy of a restaurant kitchen was not a good fit for me. I relocated to Washington, D.C., to live with my sister, Jessica. In the quiet of her dining room, I began experimenting with cake design for the first time. I played around with line and texture, developing my own techniques and aesthetic. The results were exciting, so Jessica and I decided to start a business. I photographed some cakes and built a website, while Jessica worked on a business plan and scheduled meetings with event planners. We rented a kitchen by the hour and booked a few local clients. Maybe in a few years, we thought, we might get a photo in a magazine.

But fate had something very different in mind. Two weeks after we launched the website, the *Today* show invited me to New York to participate in their popular wedding series, *Today Show Throws a Modern Wedding*. When host Gail Simmons introduced viewers to my cake design on national television, she called me "the darling of the blogosphere." Unbeknownst to us, bloggers had been taking photographs of my cakes from the website and sharing them all over the Internet. My cakes had been blogged, tweeted, pinned, and shared worldwide. Maggie Austin Cake had gone viral.

After that, business grew steadily. High-profile clients from all over the world booked me for weddings. I made sugar flowers for the White House Christmas and was featured on HGTV. I have a line of wedding cakes at the Imperial Hotel in Tokyo. I even made Dr. Jane Goodall a birthday cake!

Throughout all this, sharing what I do and how I do it is second nature. Whether in workshops or via video instruction, I find the process of passing along my craft to be both personally rewarding and professionally exciting, and it fulfills my need to connect with people who share my love of making beautiful things. And what a vibrant and diverse community it is! In my experience, a retired accountant who has never heard of gum paste is just as capable of producing a stunning sugar orchid as an executive pastry chef.

In the world of ballet, as any dancer will attest, the performance is the manifestation of the passionate and relentless pursuit of unachievable perfection. The love of the studio, the unwavering discipline, the fundamental drive to push a little further with each gesture . . . this is what you will find within these pages. And the reward? The final placement of a sugar rose, placed just so, on your very own masterpiece.

INSPIRATION

Inspiration isn't something that comes. It's something that simply *is*. Everywhere. Always. I pore over runway snapshots from Paris Fashion Week while having my morning coffee; I treat myself to an evening at the John F. Kennedy Center for the Performing Arts to see the Mariinsky Ballet perform Petipa's *Raymonda*. I have a picnic with my nieces at George Washington's River Farm estate; my husband brings home a fascinating piece of pottery from a local antique store. . . . While these small experiences may not end up translating directly into cakes, they are part of my life and therefore fundamental to my artistic expression.

I feel so fortunate to live so close to the amazing museums in Washington, D.C. I spend more time than I should simply wandering around the Renwick Gallery or the American Art Museum or the Hirshhorn Museum. I have no background in art. I've never taken an art class or studied art history. I just consider myself an appreciator. But being in the presence of masterpieces allows me to absorb a kind of visual vocabulary. In the same way an author uses individual words to write a novel, I draw upon my internal collection of visual images to create a design. My sister keeps up on all the newest exhibits, but I find myself returning to the same galleries time after time.

No matter how often I sit and contemplate van Huysum's *Still Life with Flowers and Fruit*, for example, I see something different every time. I first marveled at the movement in the painting—how the eye is guided from the grapes resting on the table up to the white parrot tulip and around to the hyacinth in a graceful arc. Then I looked at how red is interspersed throughout the arrangement, establishing a kind of balanced rhythm. From the repetition of shapes to the use of highlight and shadow, this painting is pure compositional perfection. I don't have any interest in re-creating this work, but the elegant chaos of eighteenth-century Dutch still lifes influences the choices I make when arranging my own sugar flowers.

LEFT: *Huysum, Jan van / Dutch, 1682–1749 / Still Life with Flowers and Fruit / c. 1715 / Oil on panel*
RIGHT: *Gold Leaf with Lace Overlay, page 127*

LEFT: *Monet, Claude / French, 1840–1926 / The Japanese Footbridge / c. 1899 / Oil on canvas*
RIGHT: *Impressionist Cookies, page 201*

Of all the galleries in the National Gallery of Art, I spend the most time with the Impressionists. Looking at Monet's paintings in books or online is one thing, but seeing the actual texture of each brushstroke sends chills down my spine. The layering of the colors belies both dynamic energy and extreme patience. One of my favorite paintings is of the famed Japanese Footbridge at Giverny, which Monet modeled after images from his beloved block prints in the Ukiyo-e style. I visit Tokyo frequently, and I always make time to walk in the East Garden at the Imperial Palace. The wisteria all bloom at once in late April, and it's no wonder this has been an inspiring vision for so many artists.

My curiosity takes me on adventures, sometimes to far-flung places and sometimes just through my pile of art books. Discovering the origins of inspiration for other artists unveils the universality of the visual vocabulary. We are all connected and influenced by the world around us. When I sit down with my colors and my cookies, I'm not mimicking Monet. Rather, I am bringing an aesthetic that crosses time and culture to a different (edible) medium.

Closer to home, my daily walks with my dog, Bessie, provide me with another opportunity to file away more visual information. My phone is filled with photos of sunlight filtering through leaves and strange flowers that bloomed overnight and the red tail of the neighborhood fox that's too fast for me to capture fully. Bessie sniffs the ground, covered in tufted dandelion heads, and I have my own sensory experience taking snapshots of the world around me. Not research, just presence.

Sometimes, inspiration is completely direct. Growing up in New England, I fell in love with stained glass, in the windows of drafty churches and elaborate Victorians, and even the motley collection of lamps my dad brought home from yard sales. While I can't boast of having an authentic Tiffany piece, this is one of my absolute favorite designs, which I translated onto a cake (page 186).

Of course, as a designer, my clients are my primary source of inspiration when it comes to the direction of their cake. Together, we look at linens and colors and the décor for the venue. But not all aha moments are visual. In a casual conversation following a tasting, one memorable bride mentioned that she adored sunflowers. But with an April wedding, the florist was unable to source fresh blooms. Although the bride was resigned to more conventional seasonal flowers, I suddenly knew that she needed something that was more personal. I changed my design direction altogether and instead created enormous, everlasting sunflowers for her cake. It was a perfect (and perfectly unexpected) fit.

On occasion, the cakes themselves determine their own direction. I find that if the image in my mind of the finished project is too clear, I am sometimes unsatisfied with the outcome. Conversely, if I relax and become responsive rather than directive, I feel I am fully participating in the process. I do provide clients with sketches and work with Pantone numbers and color swatches to ensure good communication. But some projects are an opportunity for me to flex my creative muscles and try something that I've never attempted before: maybe a new flower or a different medium altogether (I've only scratched the surface of working with wafer paper).

The designs in this book were photographed at Old Chapel Farm in gorgeous Loudon County, Virginia. When I first entered the chapel, I was overwhelmed by the rich layers of history. Faded stencils and crumbling plaster give way to old beams and fieldstone. Photographing the cakes inside an active restoration site felt . . . right. There are cracks and dusty corners and chipped paint. But within that disarray, I saw intrinsic beauty in the dedication to craftsmanship.

Meticulous detail defines what I do. Look closely, though, and you'll see that the designs are harmonious without being symmetrical. Just like natural flowers, mine sometimes have torn petals. Instead of repairing broken frill, I might edge it in gold. I have committed myself to following the lead of the design without focusing too much on controlling the outcome.

Each design begins as blank canvas that you will paint with your own visual vocabulary. Every gum paste rose and delicate fondant rosette will be entirely unique to you. That, in itself, is an inspiration.

HOW TO USE
THIS BOOK

Welcome!

This book is organized by technique, and each chapter includes variations on that technique. This way of organizing stems from my training as a dancer. The ritual that is classical ballet is based on a foundation of basic technical mastery. Strung together in an infinite number of ways, the individual components become seamless choreography, and suddenly, there is art. In the same spirit, you will see the elemental techniques followed by my own artistic exploration, which in some cases brings together multiple components into a seamless artistic expression.

Unlike a cookbook or instruction manual, this book is intended to be a source of inspiration rather than a template for replication. You won't find how-tos for crumb-coating or getting a smooth fondant cover or stacking tiers—there are dozens of great cake books and many online tutorials that cover those basics. Instead, the content here focuses exclusively on decorating techniques and gum paste flowers. I wrote it with all students in mind. If you are an advanced designer, you might learn different ways to approach the tools you may have been using for years and glean new ideas from my methods. You'll see my own design process in action as I evolve and explore each technique. Even the most basic hand-rolled fondant pearl can magically transform into a freshwater specimen (see page 143).

For beginning designers and anyone trying their hand at this medium for the first time, keep in mind that all these techniques can be executed on any scale, from multitiered designs to single fondant-covered tiers to sugar cookies. The four-tier Stained Glass design on page 186 is an ambitious undertaking, even for a seasoned professional. But the painting technique itself is delightfully simple, requiring only wet pigment, your fingers, and a paper towel! I'll show you how to use thin

fondant disks as "canvases" that can sit upon a cake or cookie of any size so that you can explore decorating techniques even without pro-level technical expertise.

For designers and enthusiasts of all levels, I've included a few of my favorite cake recipes, my go-to Swiss meringue buttercream, and the all-important gum paste recipe that has the flexibility and tensile strength to create lifelike sugar flowers. After teaching countless students how to make these everlasting blooms, I can say with confidence that everyone will find joy and success regardless of level of experience. All I ask is that you leave your inner self-critic at the door. In here, we embrace imperfections!

TOOLS

IT'S EASY TO GET lost in the sea of cake decorating supplies for sale. As a thrifty Yankee, I have a pretty lean collection and my staples are versatile workhorses. Here are the things I consider to be necessary basics; they can be found online or in specialty cake decorating stores.

CELBOARD: A rigid, nonporous board with grooves for flower making. This item is crucial for making leaves and individually wired petals.

CELPAD: There are two versions of this semisoft surface, and I use both. The original has holes, which allows you to make small blossoms like hydrangea. The second version (CelPad 2) doesn't have holes, but the larger surface is great for frilling and larger flower work. If you can buy only one, get the original.

CELPIN: This small modeling tool has one rounded end and one pointed end, is made from nonstick material, and comes in several sizes. The XL works as a mini rolling pin for prepping fondant and gum paste before you pass it through a pasta roller. I use the medium size for thinning and softening sugar petals.

CORNSTARCH: Dust on your work surface or hands to prevent sticking when working with fondant or gum paste. Keep it in a shaker container for easy use.

CRAFT FOAM PAD: A little craft foam square (which can be cut from a larger piece) with a hole poked through the center. I often have students who complain about having very warm hands. This can make it difficult to work with gum paste since the warmth and moisture from your hands causes the gum paste to get sticky. Place a gum paste petal set on the craft foam pad instead of your warm palm to keep things clean and cool.

CUTTERS: For cutting out fondant or gum paste shapes and in particular for making sugar flowers and leaves. There is probably a cutter for every flower variety. But I have found that a five-petal easy rose cutter can be used to make a rose, garden rose, ranunculus, gardenia, anemone, poppy, hellebore, dahlia, lisianthus, and on and on.

DRESDEN TOOL: A nonstick tool with two different curved ends. The flatter end is great for frilling and curling the edges of gum paste flower petals. The pointier side can also be used for "drawing" veins on a leaf.

EDIBLE MARKER: A marker that contains edible ink. There are several brands of edible markers with tips ranging from thick to very fine. I use AmeriColor Gourmet Writer markers and YummyArts Edible Pen Ink Marker (fine tip), both in black.

EGG WHITES: Pasteurized liquid egg whites work extremely well as an edible "glue" for gum paste.

FLORAL TAPE: For taping together floral wire for flower arranging and food-safe insertion into cake. I prefer to use white floral tape and color it with petal dust for more realistic hues.

FLORAL WIRE: For making wired sugar flowers or individual petals and leaves. The lower the gauge number, the thicker and stronger the wire. An 18-gauge wire is strong enough to support the weight of a large garden rose. A 28-gauge wire is fine enough for a delicate orchid sepal. Precut 12-inch lengths of wire are easy to cut into smaller pieces. I mostly use white for flowers and green for leaves or berries with an exposed stem.

JEM TOOL #12 (PETAL VEINER/FRILLER): This is a fantastic (and inexpensive!) all-purpose veining stick for adding detail to sugar-flower petals.

JEWELRY PLIERS: To help insert sugar flowers into a cake tier and for bending floral wire.

MOLDS: For giving highly detailed shape to gum paste or fondant. The quality of molds varies widely. Buy from a reputable brand, such as First Impressions or Stephen Benison, that uses food-grade, high-quality, flexible silicone.

PAINTBRUSHES: I prefer soft, synthetic (cheap) brushes in various sizes that I don't have to worry about ruining, since they get washed very often. Fuller, softer brushes are great for lots of even coverage using petal or luster dusts. Medium brushes are good for dusting leaves or flatter flower petals. Small, pointed brushes are good for detail work and painting.

PAPER PUNCHES: For cutting out shapes from wafer paper. These are available in a multitude of designs at your local craft store.

PAPER TOWELS: Besides the obvious cleaning uses, I often use squares of paper towels for painting. It's a step up from finger painting.

PASTA ROLLER: I use a KitchenAid pasta roller attachment to roll out thin pieces of fondant or gum paste to a precise thickness. It's a fantastic investment and a huge time (and energy) saver. Hand-crank pasta rollers do the job as well, with a little more effort, and are very cost-effective.

PETAL/LUSTER DUSTS: Available in a veritable rainbow of colors, petal/luster dusts are perfect for dusting gum paste flowers. When mixed with vodka, they form a liquid paint. While most dusts are edible, some are only suitable for decorative elements that won't be eaten, such as wired gum paste flowers.

PIZZA CUTTER: Great for cutting strips of fondant for frills.

PIPING GEL: A thick, clear, edible gel. I use this as glue. More viscous than egg white, it can be applied with precision without the risk of running. Some of my international students have a hard time sourcing clear piping gel. Royal icing would substitute nicely for most uses.

SCISSORS: Craft scissors always come in handy, particularly for cutting wafer paper. Tiny spring-action scissors are perfect for fine details such as snipping the calyx of a rose.

STYROFOAM: I use a Styrofoam cake dummy or block as a vessel for holding gum paste flowers in various stages of completion as they dry. Insert the base of the wire into the Styrofoam, allowing plenty of room between flowers to prevent breakage.

TURNTABLE: A cake decorating must for rotating tiers with ease while working. Heavier cast-iron turntables will last for years, but inexpensive plastic ones will do the trick.

VEGETABLE SHORTENING: Use as a conditioner for gum paste and fondant and to help prevent stickiness when mixing in gel color, which can make the fondant or gum paste tacky. A bit of shortening will also give you a nonstick work surface.

WIRE CUTTERS: Heavy-duty wire cutters make easy work of cutting multiple floral wires at a time.

ZIP-TOP BAGS: Essential for storing gum paste, fondant, or in-progress decorations to keep them from drying out.

WORKING WITH FONDANT

People have strong opinions on fondant, whether that means peeling off an inch of stiff, sickly sweet sugar paste at a childhood birthday party and leaving it on the plate or secretly stealing (and eating) fondant roses from a multitiered wedding cake before it gets cut. But fondant has come a long way in quality and selection. In the hands of skilled professionals, it is rolled very thin and the cake is covered, delivered, and consumed within 24 hours. The soft, fresh fondant layer is a completely neutral canvas for decorating on all my cakes. I prefer an imported Swiss fondant rolled to just under $1/16$ inch, as it's important to me that this layer not have any impact on the flavor profile of the cake and buttercream beneath.

TIPS

- Be at peace with buying premade fondant. It is too messy and too inconsistent to make at home. Another reason I like premade fondant? It's vegetarian. Most homemade fondant recipes are made with marshmallows, which contain gelatin.

- Knead the fondant before rolling it out to make it smooth and soft. The warmth from your hands will get it to a nice workable temperature.

- Make sure you have all your tools at hand before you start rolling out the fondant. This includes your fondant smoothers, pizza cutter for trimming excess fondant, and offset spatula to help move the cake tier.

- Pull your cake tier directly from the refrigerator when you are ready to begin decorating. I prefer to chill mine overnight. The tier should be firm and covered with a thin but opaque layer of buttercream (see page 56 for information on Swiss meringue buttercream).

- When rolling the fondant, use plenty of cornstarch on your work surface to prevent sticking, and roll the fondant to about $1/16$ inch thick.

- When covering a cake tier, I like to roll out a very generous circle of fondant so I don't need to worry about coming up short as I cover the tier. This also helps to prevent pleating as I drape.

- If you find that your fondant smoothers are sticking as you work, a light dusting of cornstarch will keep everything gliding along.

- Fondant is sensitive to temperature and humidity. Too warm or humid means a sweaty, sticky canvas (not good). A cold cake is a happy cake. The ideal decorating environment has plenty of air-conditioning and a dehumidifier.

- Keep unused fondant in an airtight container or zip-top bag. To rejuvenate slightly dry or cold fondant, knead it thoroughly, using the heat of your hands and a tiny bit of vegetable shortening to soften it. The shortening will prevent it from sticking to your hands. Prep your fondant in this way to make it smooth and supple before beginning any project, whether you're covering a cake or just pressing it into a mold.

- If your design requires extra strength, or if you're working in a humid environment, mix equal parts fondant and gum paste. A lot of my techniques suggest this 50/50 option for its strength, extensibility, and quicker drying time. For example, frills made from only fondant can wilt after an hour at an outdoor summer wedding; made with a 50/50 mix of fondant and gum paste, they'll keep their shape. However, 100% gum paste is not pleasant to bite into, as it's very hard once it's dry. Save pure gum paste for wired flowers that will be removed before slicing. Anything on the surface of the cake that could end up on the plate should be a mix. Be sure your gum paste is made with pasteurized egg whites to avoid any food safety worries (see page 39 for my recipe).

- You'll find examples of tiny cakes (serving 1 or 2) in this book. Instead of enrobing the tiny tiers, I keep them "nude" and simply add a disk of fondant on top. The beauty of this is that the decorated fondant disks can be made in advance and stored in an airtight container. Spread a thin layer of buttercream on the topmost cake layer before applying the disk; the moisture from the buttercream will soften the fondant just in time for serving.

ROLLING OUT FONDANT OR GUM PASTE

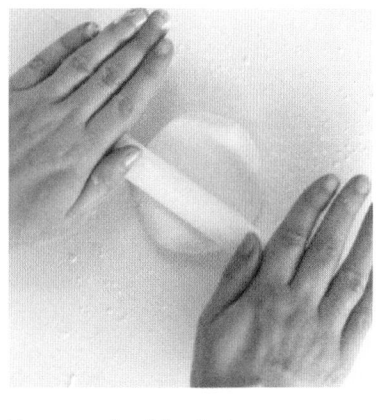

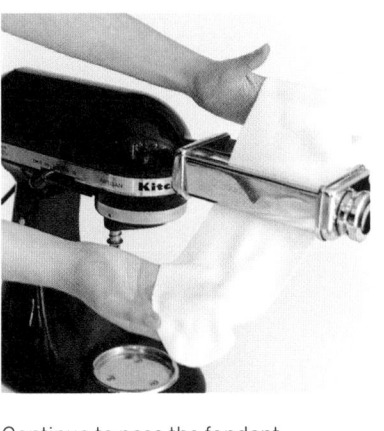

You can roll out fondant or gum paste using a rolling pin or CelPin XL.

I like to roll fondant and gum paste through a pasta roller for even thickness. Pass a small piece through the machine, starting on the widest setting (on mine, a KitchenAid stand mixer attachment, level 1).

Continue to pass the fondant through the pasta roller, increasing the thinness setting, until it is very thin, generally level 5 or 6 for most projects.

CREATING TEXTURES & SHAPES

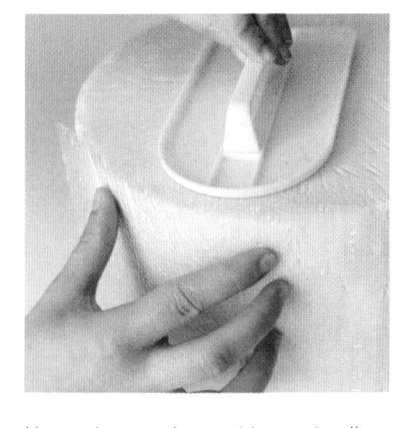

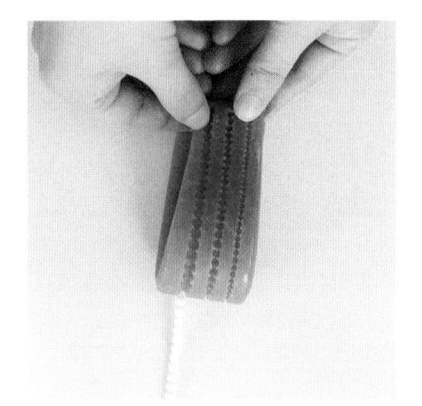

Use an impression mat to create all-over texture on a fondant surface. Be sure to do this as soon as the cake is covered, while the fondant is still fresh. A fondant smoother helps to gently hold the tier in place as you apply the impression.

Press fondant or gum paste into a silicone mold to create three-dimensional shapes. To release the fondant or gum paste, turn the mold over and carefully peel it back, allowing the piece to come out on its own. If you are using a silicone mold for the first time, season it with a tiny bit of vegetable shortening to help prevent sticking.

Strands of fondant or gum paste pearls can also be made using a silicone mold. A tiny bit of shortening rubbed into the mold will help the pearls release.

WORKING WITH GUM PASTE

There is no substitute for homemade gum paste, a soft sugar paste with an added gum agent. It's inexpensive, quick and easy to make, and far superior to anything you can buy. Soft, extensible, and resilient when fresh, it hardens and keeps its shape when dry, so it's magic for flower making. (Fondant, on the other hand, has no gum additive and therefore lacks strength and stretch.) However, even though it's technically edible, gum paste is not pleasant to eat, so don't use 100% gum paste for any decoration (frills, appliqués, molds, etc.) that could end up on your plate—opt for fondant or a 50/50 mix of fondant and gum paste instead. This recipe is precise, so be sure to use a digital scale to measure the ingredients.

TIPS

- There are a variety of gum additives available in the marketplace, but this recipe is specific to tylose, which I prefer for its whiteness and consistent performance. You can find it in specialty cake decorating stores and online.

- To color the entire batch of gum paste, gel paste color can be added during the mixing process before the tylose goes in.

- If you don't want to color the entire batch, the finished gum paste can be colored by massaging in gel paste color (as shown on page 44). Use a bit of shortening on your work surface to prevent sticking. A pair of disposable gloves comes in handy if you want to avoid staining your hands.

- Gum paste dries out ridiculously fast. If you are thinning rose petals and pause to pour yourself a glass of water in the next room, by the time you get back, you can go ahead and throw out that petal set. Plan accordingly! Always keep gum paste in a tightly sealed zip-top bag when not in use, and work with only one small piece at a time. An airtight bag won't keep the gum paste soft permanently, but it'll buy you a bit of time as you work.

- If I'm working on a project over a few days, I keep the batch of gum paste tightly sealed at room temperature.

- Always bring stored gum paste all the way to room temperature and give it a mini massage (with a tiny bit of shortening if it feels dry) before using; the heat of your hands will soften it and make it workable.

- Cornstarch will help prevent the gum paste from sticking to your hands. Keep some at the ready in a shaker, especially if you have very warm hands. A light dusting of cornstarch on the surface of the gum paste will also prevent it from sticking as you roll it through the pasta roller.

- You can mix in a portion of gum paste (no more than 50%) to fondant to give extra strength to decorative elements applied to a cake's surface.

HOMEMADE
GUM PASTE

MAKES
about 1 pound

75 g egg whites
382 g confectioners' sugar
19 g tylose powder
12 g vegetable shortening

1 In the bowl of a stand mixer fitted with the paddle attachment, combine the egg whites and confectioners' sugar and mix on medium speed for about 2 minutes. The mixture should be glossy and smooth.

2 Reduce the mixer speed to medium-low, add the tylose, and mix until fully incorporated. Raise the speed to medium and mix until smooth. This should take no more than 15 seconds.

3 Scrape the gum paste out onto a nonporous work surface. Knead in all the shortening. Store in a zip-top bag. Double-wrap and refrigerate for up to two weeks if not using within 2 or 3 days. Gum paste can also be frozen for up to 6 months.

WORKING WITH WAFER PAPER

Wafer paper is a delicate edible sheet of pressed starch, usually rice- or potato-based. It is slightly translucent, rather brittle, and extremely versatile. As it is an increasingly popular product for cake decoration, the availability of wafer paper in a variety colors and even patterns is expanding. I've only just begun my own exploration into this new (to me) medium, and I'm excited to discover what it can do.

I use two different techniques when working with rice paper. The first is to cut out shapes, either using one of the many beautiful paper punches available in crafts stores or by cutting out a pattern or freehand design with scissors. The second is to steam the paper to soften it and then bend and shape it into more fluid, softer forms. To do this, carefully hold the paper near a source of steam, such as a steamer or kettle of boiling water.

TIPS
- Brush petal dust over a sheet of wafer paper to add natural-looking color that still has some translucency. If you are planning to steam the paper, brush the shapes with color after steaming, not before.

- Wafer paper is extremely sensitive to moisture. I use piping gel to glue wafer-paper elements, as I find that plain water dissolves the paper far too quickly.

- Steaming wafer paper is an exercise in restraint! The transformation between a stiff piece of paper and a collapsed, soggy mess happens in seconds. Be patient and be sure you have lots of extra paper on hand. Don't hold the paper too close to the origin of the steam. Rotate it constantly to avoid it folding in on itself. For a more natural look, gently rub the edge as it's being steamed.

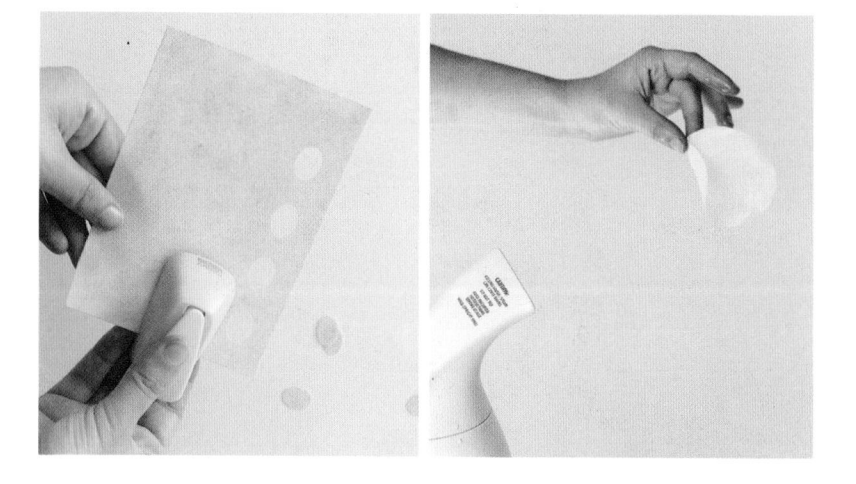

WORKING WITH EDIBLE CAKE LACE

Edible sugar lace is a relative newcomer to the cake-decorating world. It's a remarkably fine and flexible medium made from sugar and some sort of gum additive and shaped by spreading it over a silicone mat, and it is capable of taking on an extreme level of detail. It comes premixed and is easy to use. There are several brands readily available, and I've had the greatest success with Claire Bowman's Cake Lace. Just follow the instructions on the package and away you go!

TIPS

- The cake lace mixture is best used with silicone mats that are designed specifically for it. The mats are thin, flexible, and have incredible detail, and are a bit pricey. Make sure you really like the pattern before you purchase!

- The mixture can be colored using gel colors before being spread over the mat. Alternatively, petal or luster dust can be brushed over the top of the dry lace.

- Even though the lace is designed to be somewhat flexible, it is still brittle and needs to be handled with care. Always make a few extra pieces in case of breakage.

- Cake lace can be made in advance and placed in a container between layers of waxed paper until ready to be used.

- Some mats have a distinct borderlike appearance, with a continuous pattern. Others have individual shapes that can be extracted. Either way, I like to break up the pieces and reconfigure them in different ways to make the design unique each time.

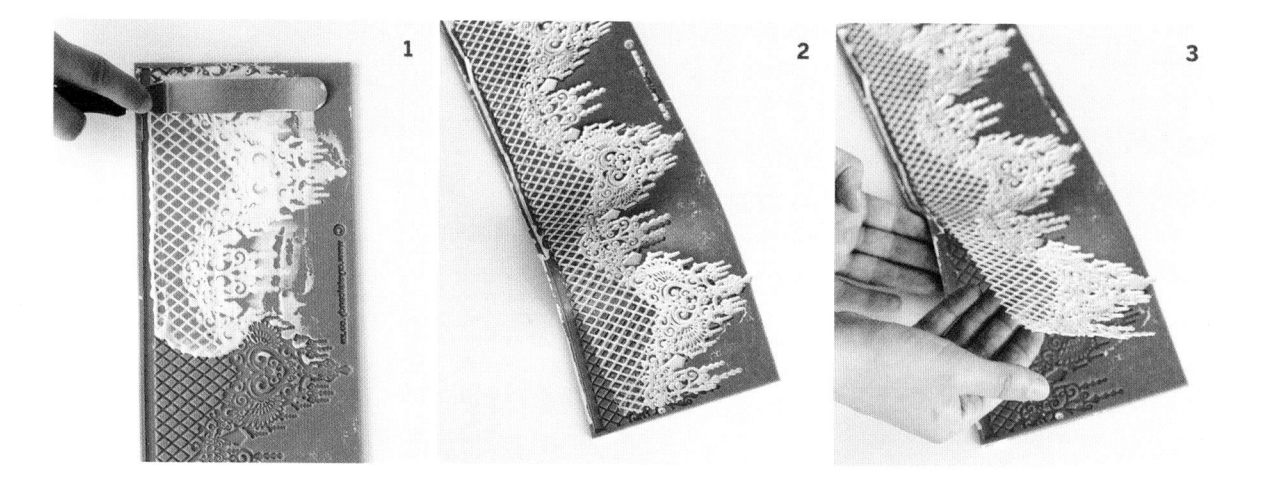

COLOR

Just as the placement of shapes can direct the eye, so, too, can color. A riot of primary hues is the right choice for my bold Frida Kahlo–inspired design on page 130, but the muted pale gray offsetting the gentle pink of the dahlia on page 72 quietly asks the viewer to contemplate the light texture of the frills and curve of the petals. Unexpected uses of pigment, like dark brown petal dust brushed on the surface of a silvery green leaf, give a sense of realism and dimension to my work. From painting on cakes to mixing the perfect ombré fondant, the use of color can enrich designs in endless ways.

Color is incredibly subjective—not only in what we like, but even in what we see and how we identify color. I once had a design meeting with a couple who told me they wanted a fuchsia cake. As the three of us sat there with my portfolio, we each pointed to a different example of what "fuchsia" looked like. At that point, I brought out a Pantone booklet and we settled on a number, rather than a name.

TIPS
- Event planners or designers may be familiar with Pantone numbers, but your client may not be. Ask for a swatch of fabric from the bridesmaid's dress or paint chips from a hardware store. Not only does this help you, the designer, to have a physical piece from which to color match, but it gives the client a tool to communicate clearly.

- Gel color is the way to go for coloring fondant or gum paste. Massage the gel into the fondant or gum paste, adding it only a little at a time, until you reach your desired color. Some colors can stain your hands, so have some disposable gloves handy. Use a dab of shortening on the work surface as you massage in color, as the gel makes the fondant or gum paste sticky.

- If you need to match a specific color, try your blend of gel colors on a small piece of fondant or gum paste first. Once you have your formula down, color the entire batch.

- Freshly colored fondant or gum paste intensifies as it sits. The red fondant you thought was not quite deep enough might be perfect after it has rested in a zip-top bag for 20 minutes.

- On the other hand, as soon as colored fondant is exposed to air and light, it starts a slow color fade. Direct sunlight and fluorescent light accelerate this process. Colored gum paste is more fade resistant.

- There are tons of color dusts available, and you could spend a fortune on them. Use these to brush soft color onto gum paste flowers or for wet medium paint (see below). Just as with fine art pigments, edible colors can be layered and blended to make new ones, meaning you don't necessarily need to buy orange petal dust if you have red and yellow.

- Clear, high-proof alcohol or extract turns dry pigments into an edible paint. The higher the proof, the more quickly it evaporates, leaving only the color behind. I use (cheap) vodka that I would not be tempted to drink. It imparts no flavor or odor or quantifiable alcohol.

- Read the labels. There are some dusts, particularly metallic ones, that are meant for decorative use only. Save these for "display only" cakes or for elements that will be removed from the cake before serving.

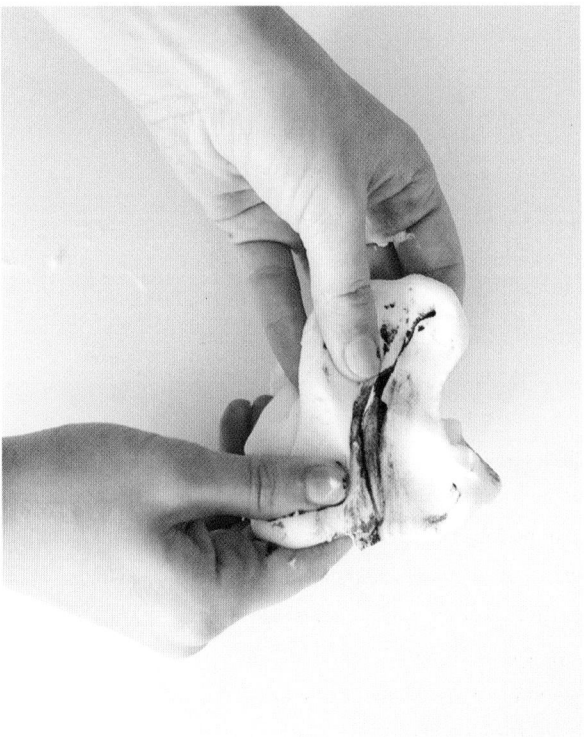 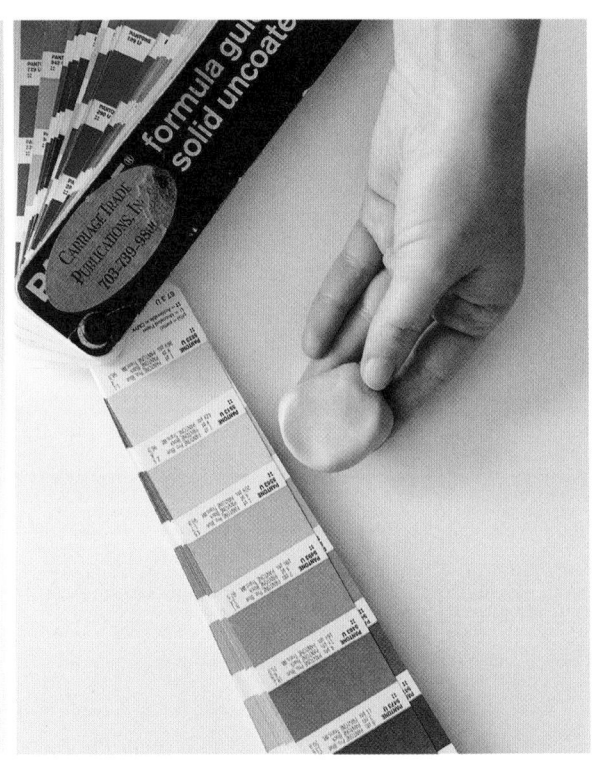

LEFT: *Mix gel color into fondant or gum paste. It can get messy! Wear gloves if you'd prefer to avoid stained fingers.*
RIGHT: *I test out a turquoise color match using my faithful Pantone book.*

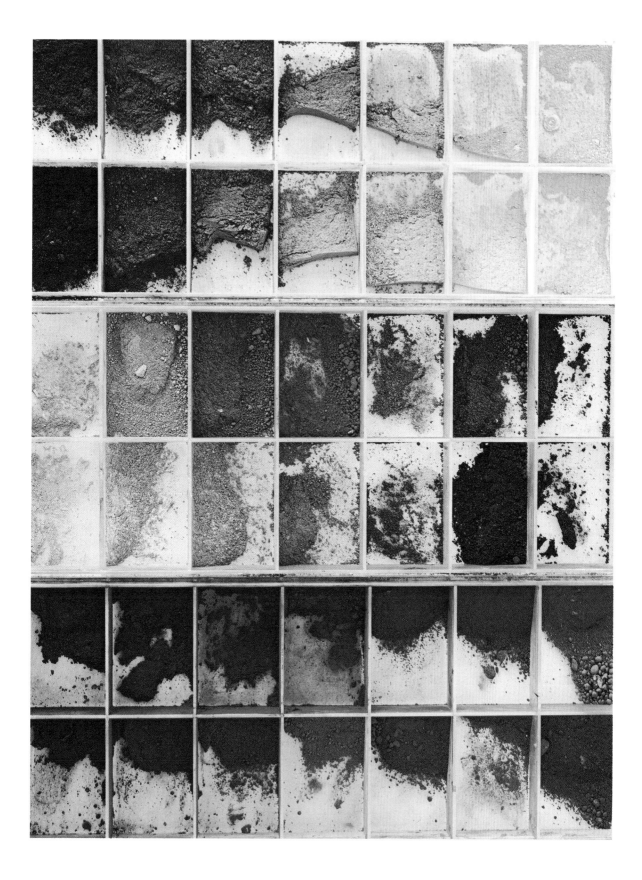

RECIPES

"TOO PRETTY TO EAT" may be the most common comment I get. I firmly disagree! Cake is meant to be eaten. It's a joy and a gift to be able to pass on my work to a client for them to enjoy with friends and family. The same attention to detail that goes into the outside of the cake is also found on the inside. The recipes I use do not yield cakes that can handle being carved into shapes, nor do they have an indefinite shelf life. They are, at their core, home recipes.

Beneath any of my fondant-draped tiers, you will find four layers of cake alternating with frosting, with endless flavor compositions. Chocolate cake paired with hazelnut praline and cappuccino buttercream, pear cake with blackberry and white chocolate buttercream, Fiori di Sicilia–scented vanilla cake with milk chocolate Earl Grey buttercream . . . Here are a few of my favorite recipes for cake, buttercream, and cookies to help get you started exploring the techniques and ideas in this book.

TIPS • When I was attending the French Pastry School, the answer to "How long does this take to bake?" was often "As long as it takes until it's done." Timers were not commonly used. We learned to use our senses to determine when things were ready to come out. Think of the times attached to these recipes as guides only. Every oven is different; use a thermometer that sits in your oven rather than relying on the oven's gauge. The easiest way to tell if a cake is done is to poke a skewer into the center. It should come out clean. There's also a bit of leeway with oven temperature. I find that 350°F crisps the edges of my chocolate cake ever so slightly, so I've lowered it to 340°F.

• I like to bake taller layers, as I always trim the tops and bottoms. It's a little extra time and cake, but worth it. So my recipes are based on 3-inch-tall pans. If you are using 2-inch-tall pans, I recommend only filling the pan about two-thirds full or using a pan that is 1 inch larger in diameter.

• I use the shortcut of baking spray with flour to prepare my pans, but you could also butter and flour them, which will work just as well.

• After baking, I let the cake sit in the pan for 20 to 30 minutes before inverting it. Once completely cool, wrap the cake tightly with plastic wrap. Let the cake sit in the fridge overnight before slicing and/or eating for best workability and flavor. For longer-term storage, keep it in the freezer.

To Make Mini Cakes

Bake the cake batter in a 12 x 18 x 1-inch rimmed baking sheet. Once cooled, slice the cake horizontally into two ½-inch-tall layers and use a cookie cutter to cut out mini cake layers. A 2½-inch round cutter will yield about 16 mini cakes with 3 layers each. Fill in between the layers as desired and spread a thin, even layer of buttercream on the top. Place the finished cakes on a cake board or baking sheet and chill until firm before wrapping tightly with plastic wrap; they should be kept in the fridge or freezer until ready to be adorned with a decorated fondant plaque (as on pages 181, 199, and 221).

Simple Syrup

1 cup (200 g) sugar / 1 cup (236 g) water

In a small saucepan, combine the sugar and water and bring to a boil over medium-high heat, stirring occasionally to help the sugar dissolve. Remove from the heat and let cool completely.

THIS IS PRETTY DECADENT. There's a lot of fat in here, and it's coming from multiple sources—butter, oil, and eggs. That being said, this cake is magically tender and not at all dense. The addition of the Fiori di Sicilia, an Italian extract bursting with floral, citrus, and vanilla aromas, makes it very special. The ⅛ teaspoon in the recipe is just enough to get your attention; add up to ¼ teaspoon for something more dramatic. It's not a grocery store find, but it is available at some specialty food stores as well as online.

VANILLA CAKE

MAKES
two 6-inch round cake layers

Baking spray with flour, for the pans

1¼ cups (150 g) all-purpose flour

1½ cups (180 g) cake flour

1¾ cups plus 2 tablespoons (375 g) sugar

1¼ teaspoons baking powder

½ teaspoon baking soda

¾ teaspoon fine sea salt

½ cup plus 1 tablespoon (114 g) vegetable oil

3 whole large eggs (150 g)

1 large egg white (32 g)

½ cup (58 g) buttermilk

1 cup (228 g) sour cream

1 tablespoon vanilla bean paste

⅛ teaspoon Fiori Di Sicilia extract

¾ cup (1½ sticks/170 g) unsalted butter, at room temperature (see Note)

1　Preheat the oven to 325°F. Spray two 6 by 3-inch round baking pans with baking spray with flour.

2　In the bowl of a stand mixer fitted with the paddle attachment, combine the all-purpose flour, cake flour, sugar, baking powder, baking soda, and salt. Mix on low speed for about 30 seconds. In a separate bowl, whisk together the oil, eggs, egg white, buttermilk, sour cream, vanilla, and Fiori di Sicilia.

3　Break the butter into small pieces and, with the mixer on low speed, add the butter to the dry ingredients piece by piece. Once all the butter has been added, the mixture should look sandy. Raise the mixer speed to medium-low and slowly stream in the wet ingredients, pausing halfway through to scrape down the sides of the bowl. Raise the mixer speed to medium-high and beat for 30 to 45 seconds.

4　Divide the batter between the prepared pans and bake for about 55 minutes, or until a skewer inserted into a cake comes out clean. Let the cakes cool in the pans for 20 to 30 minutes before inverting onto wire racks to cool completely.

NOTE　*Be sure your butter is very soft. When pressed, your finger should go right into it. Use the defrost setting on your microwave to speed up the process as necessary.*

Buttercream Pairing

APRICOT PRESERVES & ALMOND BUTTERCREAM

1 recipe plain Swiss Meringue Buttercream (page 56)

2 teaspoons vanilla bean paste

¼ teaspoon almond extract

Pinch of fine sea salt

¼ cup (85 g) apricot preserves

Simple Syrup (page 49), for brushing

1 Put the plain buttercream in a medium bowl and mix in the vanilla bean paste, almond extract, and salt.

2 Transfer 1 cup of the flavored buttercream to a medium bowl. Add the apricot preserves and mix well.

3 Brush the cake layers with cooled simple syrup to keep them extra moist.

4 Pipe a "dam" of the almond buttercream around the edge of the bottom cake layer. Fill it with the apricot mixture.

5 Add the next cake layer and coat it with a layer of almond buttercream only. Add another cake layer, fill with the apricot mixture, and top with the final cake layer, then frost the top and sides of the cake with the remaining almond buttercream.

THIS CAKE IS SUPER MOIST and extremely chocolaty with the flavor bolstered by a full cup of coffee. I prefer a blend of Dutched and natural cocoas for a balance of flavor and a deep, rich color. Hershey's Special Dark brand is a 50/50 mix; or use equal amounts of your favorite brands. Be sure the coffee is hot, freshly brewed, and of good quality, as the flavor will come through in the cake. No skimping with instant.

CHOCOLATE CAKE

MAKES
two 6-inch round cake layers

Baking spray with flour, for the pans

1¾ cups (227 g) all-purpose flour

2 cups (400 g) sugar

6 tablespoons (30 g) Dutch process cocoa powder

6 tablespoons (30 g) unsweetened natural cocoa powder

1 teaspoon baking powder

2 teaspoons baking soda

1¼ teaspoons fine sea salt

½ cup plus 1 tablespoon (114 g) vegetable oil

¾ cup (173 g) full-fat buttermilk

¼ cup (57 g) sour cream

2 large eggs (100 g)

1¼ teaspoons vanilla bean paste

1 cup (230 g) hot coffee (see Note)

1 Preheat the oven to 340°F. Spray two 6 by 3-inch round baking pans with baking spray with flour.

2 In the bowl of a stand mixer fitted with the paddle attachment, combine the flour, sugar, cocoa powders, baking powder, baking soda, and salt. Mix on low speed for about 30 seconds. In a separate bowl, whisk together the oil, buttermilk, sour cream, eggs, and vanilla bean paste.

3 With the mixer running on low speed, add the wet mixture to the dry and mix just until combined. Carefully stream in the hot coffee and mix until combined, pausing once to scrape down the sides of the bowl. The batter will look very runny.

4 Divide the batter between the prepared pans and bake for about 45 minutes, or until a skewer inserted into a cake comes out clean. Let the cakes cool in the pans for 20 to 30 minutes before inverting onto wire racks to cool completely.

NOTE *Make sure this is 1 cup of coffee in a liquid measuring cup, not 1 cup on your coffeepot.*

Buttercream Pairing

BUTTERSCOTCH AND TOFFEE

1 cup (200 g) butterscotch chips

1 recipe plain Swiss Meringue Buttercream (page 56)

Pinch of salt

6 tablespoons (42 g) crushed toffee pieces

1 In the top of a double boiler or in a heatproof bowl set over a saucepan of simmering water (the bowl should not touch the water), melt the butterscotch chips, stirring often. Butterscotch melts fairly quickly and needs to be stirred often to prevent scorching. (Alternatively, melt the butterscotch chips in a bowl in the microwave.) Remove from the heat.

2 Temper the melted butterscotch by adding about ½ cup of the buttercream, stirring vigorously until smooth. This helps prevent the butterscotch from seizing and forming little chunks.

3 Add the butterscotch-buttercream mixture to the remaining plain buttercream, add the salt, and mix well.

4 Pipe or spread the buttercream on the bottom cake layer. Sprinkle about 2 tablespoons (14 g) crushed toffee pieces on top, avoiding the outermost edge of the buttercream.

5 Repeat with the remaining cake layers, omitting the toffee on the top layer. Frost the top and sides of the cake with the remaining buttercream.

EACH YEAR FOR HER birthday, my sister (and business partner), Jess, requests carrot cake—no walnuts, heavy on the cream cheese frosting. I'm including optional walnuts in this recipe, but be sure to check with your loved ones first for their preference. I learned my lesson after watching Jess painstakingly pick out each and every piece of walnut. The splash of whiskey in the cream cheese frosting helped to smooth things over.

CARROT CAKE

MAKES
two 6-inch round cake layers

3 cups (300 g) shredded carrots
(from 5 medium; I buy bagged shredded
carrots from the grocery store)

2 cups (260 g) all-purpose flour

1¾ teaspoons baking powder

1¾ teaspoons baking soda

½ teaspoon fine sea salt

1½ teaspoons ground cinnamon

¼ teaspoon ground allspice

¼ teaspoon freshly grated nutmeg

¼ teaspoon ground cloves

¼ teaspoon ground ginger

4 large eggs (200 g)

2 cups (400 g) sugar

1 tablespoon vanilla bean paste

½ cup (100 g) vegetable oil

¾ cup (170 g) sour cream

1 cup (115 g) chopped walnuts (optional)

1 Preheat the oven to 350°F. Spray two 6- by 3-inch round baking pans with baking spray with flour.

2 Place the shredded carrots in a food processor and pulse a few times so the pieces are small and fairly uniform. Lay the carrots out on several pieces of paper towel and pat to absorb excess moisture. Set aside to dry.

3 In a medium bowl, whisk together the flour, baking powder, baking soda, salt, and spices. In a separate large bowl, whisk together the eggs, sugar, vanilla, oil, and sour cream. Toss the carrots in the dry ingredients so that they are completely coated. Whisk the wet ingredients into the dry ingredients, scraping down the sides of the bowl as needed. Add the walnuts (if using) and mix just to combine.

4 Divide the batter between the prepared pans. Bake for about 55 minutes, or until a skewer inserted into a cake comes out clean. Let the cakes cool in the pans for 20 to 30 minutes before inverting onto wire racks to cool completely.

Buttercream Pairing

WHISKEY-SOAKED LAYERS & VANILLA BEAN–CREAM CHEESE BUTTERCREAM

¼ cup (28 g) whiskey

3 tablespoons Simple Syrup (page 49)

12 ounces (340 g) cream cheese, at room temperature

1 recipe plain Swiss Meringue Buttercream (page 56)

2 teaspoons vanilla bean paste

Pinch of salt

1 Mix the whiskey and simple syrup together and brush generously on all the cake layers. Allow it to soak in for about 1 minute before brushing on more if you want a stronger flavor.

2 In the bowl of a stand mixer fitted with the paddle attachment, beat the cream cheese on medium-high speed until fluffy. Reduce the speed to medium-low and add the buttercream in small amounts until fully incorporated.

3 Mix in the vanilla bean paste and salt.

4 Assemble, fill, and frost the cake with the vanilla bean–cream cheese buttercream.

I DON'T OFFER BUTTERCREAM-ONLY cakes, because there is relatively little to be done with buttercream in the way of intricate, modern cake decoration. (And to be perfectly honest, I'm lousy with a piping bag.) But I love its silky mouthfeel and rich taste, and always include a layer underneath a cake's fondant and in between the cake layers. Swiss meringue buttercream is my pick both to work with and to eat. I prefer to use liquid pasteurized egg whites because it's easy and they're food-safe, but since the egg whites and sugar cook together over a double boiler, this recipe is food-safe even with unpasteurized eggs. Because there are so few ingredients, the butter itself plays a major role in the flavor profile. Find a brand or purveyor whose product remains consistent throughout the year. I prefer butter without a very strong dairy or grass flavor so that the flavorings I add come through clearly. The most common cause of an unfortunate buttercream experience is butter that is either too warm or too cold. If you haven't set it out in advance, the defrost setting on your microwave is a great way to bring butter to room temperature.

SWISS MERINGUE BUTTERCREAM

MAKES *5 cups, enough to comfortably fill and frost a 6-inch round cake or tier*

4–5 large egg whites (140g)

1 cup (200 g) sugar

¼ teaspoon cream of tartar

1 pound (4 sticks/454 g) unsalted butter, cut into cubes, at room temperature

1 Set a heatproof bowl over a saucepan of simmering water; the bottom of the bowl should not touch the water. In the bowl, whisk together the egg whites, sugar, and cream of tartar until the mixture reaches 160°F. Pass the mixture through a fine-mesh strainer into the bowl of a stand mixer.

2 Fit the mixer with the whisk attachment and whip on high speed until stiff peaks form and the outside of the mixer bowl has cooled to room temperature. Use this time to be sure the butter is at room temperature.

3 Switch to the paddle attachment, set the mixer to low speed, and slowly add the butter cubes, one at a time. Don't panic when the buttercream goes through a curdled-looking phase. Everything will smooth out with the last few cubes of butter. You may increase the speed to medium once all the butter has been added, but any higher will cause air pockets to form. Buttercream can be used immediately, refrigerated in an airtight container for up to 1 week, or frozen for up to 2 months.

TIPS
- A double batch of this recipe fits in a standard 5-quart KitchenAid mixer. For the first year and half of my business, I made all my cakes with one KitchenAid.

- A broken-looking finished product usually means something was at the wrong temperature. If the buttercream is soupy looking, grab an ice pack from the freezer, place it around the bowl, and let the mixer run for several minutes. Conversely, if there are visible pieces of butter and the bowl is cold to the touch, remove the bowl and carefully run the outside of the bowl, toward the base, under hot water for 5 seconds before returning it to the mixer.

- Keep in mind that added extracts, liqueur, melted chocolate, or fruit purees may change the consistency or stability of your buttercream. It's helpful to pipe a "dam" of plain or vanilla buttercream around the edge of a cake layer to keep a loose or slightly unstable filling in place within your tier.

- I finish my cakes with a thin but opaque layer of buttercream and let them sit overnight in the fridge before draping them with fondant. The firmer and colder the cake, the easier it is to cover.

A GOOD SUGAR COOKIE is a perfect vehicle for decoration. But the tastier and more tender the cookie, the more it spreads like crazy in the oven. Conversely, the cookie that doesn't grow a millimeter in the oven tends to lack the tender, buttery reason you want to eat it. This recipe achieves the right balance, for a delicious cookie that still holds its shape.

ROLLED SUGAR COOKIES

MAKES
several dozen cookies

1 pound (4 sticks/454 g) unsalted butter, cut into cubes, at room temperature

2 cups (400 g) sugar

2 large eggs (100 g), at room temperature

1 teaspoon vanilla extract

2 teaspoons vanilla bean paste

6 cups (780 g) all-purpose flour, plus more for dusting

1 tablespoon baking powder

1 teaspoon sea salt

1 In the bowl of a stand mixer fitted with the paddle attachment, cream the butter and sugar on medium-high speed until light and fluffy. Mix in the eggs, vanilla extract, and vanilla bean paste. Scrape down the sides of the bowl.

2 In a separate bowl, sift together the flour, baking powder, and salt. With the mixer on low speed, slowly add the dry ingredients to the butter mixture and mix until fully incorporated.

3 Turn out the dough onto plastic wrap and pat it down into a round. Wrap tightly and refrigerate for at least 1 hour before rolling out. (At this point the dough can be refrigerated, tightly wrapped, for up to 1 week or frozen for up to 2 months.)

4 When you are ready to bake, preheat the oven to 325°F. Line several baking sheets with parchment paper.

5 Dust your work surface with plenty of flour. Roll out the dough to about ¼ inch thick—if the dough is too cold, it will be too firm to roll; too warm, it will stick to your work surface and not cut cleanly. Use plenty of flour on your work surface as you roll out the dough. Cut the dough into shapes and place them on the prepared baking sheets. Set in the freezer for at least 15 minutes to help prevent spreading. Bake for 15 to 20 minutes, depending on size, until golden. Let cool completely before decorating.

TIPS

- When working with decorated cookies, it's important that the cookie is substantial enough (¼ inch thick) to support the weight of the decoration, but also to make for a pleasant eating experience (too much fondant and too little cookie is not a good combination).

- When rolling a fondant canvas for your cookie, a thinness of level 4 on a pasta roller (about $\frac{1}{16}$ inch thick) is a good compromise between as thin as possible but still thick enough to be able to be brushed gently (stretched) to the edge of the cookie.

- You can attach fondant to your cookie using water, but using a flavored simple syrup (see page 49) or liqueur instead is not only tasty, but also extends the cookie's shelf life.

- Fully decorated cookies freeze quite well! When thawing, be sure they are not stacked or touching, and leave them alone as condensation occurs and dissipates. If you touch a painted surface while wet, the paint will smudge. Let air-dry completely before handling.

FRILLS

The first time I covered a cake tier in frills way back in
2010, I had no idea that it would be the start
of a trend. A single frill used as a border is a classic
decorating method, but frills en masse take on a very
different personality. They can be pleated or
papery, in rows or rolled, flat or gathered.

OMBRÉ
Frills

PAPER-THIN FRILLS ARE THE perfect medium for a soft ombré effect. The color transition is seamless and the texture is captivating. The secret to such a light and airy look is far from conventional. The rows are applied upside down so the frills can "open" ever so slightly once the cake is upright. Using a 50/50 mix of fondant and gum paste instead of pure fondant gives the frills more strength to stand up to humidity. I allowed for a large difference in diameter between the two tiers to leave room for the large sugar-flower arrangement. Peonies, ranunculi, and roses in hues pulled from the same pink palette create a cohesive look. (See sugar flower instructions beginning on page 224.)

cake pan

cornstarch

water

Dresden tool

pizza cutter

Cel Pad 2

TOOLS

- Bench scraper
- Fondant or a 50/50 mix of fondant and gum paste in desired colors (here, dusty rose and white)
- Zip-top bags
- Cake pan(s) in the same size as the cake tier(s)
- Fondant-covered cake tier(s), cold and firm
- Turntable
- Pasta roller
- Cornstarch in shaker
- Pizza cutter
- CelPad 2 (no holes)
- Dresden tool
- Small paintbrush
- Small dish of water
- Paper towel

fondant covered cake tier

fondant

turntable

bench scraper

1   Using the bench scraper, cut the colored fondant in half. Set one half aside; this will be your darkest color. Cut the remaining half into six equal portions (it's okay to eyeball this!). Divide the white fondant into three equal portions. Pair the white pieces with decreasing proportions of the colored pieces to make the different shades.

2   Knead each section to create the different levels of saturations. An ombré design can contain as many or as few values as you wish. It will depend on how dark you start and how light you finish, as well as how gradual you wish the transition to be. Always keep a sample of the "mother" color (the most saturated) in case you need to create more of a color along the ombré line. Work with one small piece at a time and store the other fondant pieces in zip-top bags until they are needed.

3   Place the cake pan on top of the cake tier. Hold one hand inside the pan and one hand underneath the cake tier, apply firm pressure between your hands so that the pan doesn't slide, and then invert the cake in one swift movement. This is scary, but it will be okay! My husband helps me with cakes larger than 13 inches, as they get too heavy for me to flip; you may need to enlist someone to help you.

4   Center the inverted cake tier on the turntable. Check to be sure the cake is still even on the pan. Adjust as necessary.

5 Beginning with a small amount of the lightest color, use a pasta roller to roll the fondant to a thinness of level 6 as described on page 37. Lightly dust the fondant with cornstarch as needed to prevent stickiness. Using the pizza cutter, cut strips about 6 inches long and about ¾ inch wide (anything longer will be too difficult to work with). The scraps can be massaged a bit and rerolled if necessary. You can place the strips in a zip-top bag when not in use, but I don't recommend cutting and storing more than about ten strips at a time. Even in a bag, they will dry out. You will need ten to thirteen rows of frills per tier. The transition from one color to the next can happen anytime you wish, but if you'd like to be a bit more precise, divide the number of rows by the number of shades in your ombré design; this cake features two to three rows of frills per color value.

6 Place the first strip on the CelPad. Dust the fingers of your nondominant hand with a bit of cornstarch and place them firmly on the top of the strip. Hold the Dresden tool like a pencil and work with the duller, flatter side. Starting about ¼ inch from the top of the strip, pull the tip of the Dresden tool down all the way past the edge to create a thin, ruffled edge. If you stop pulling before you reach the edge of the strip, you will simply build up the fondant, creating a thicker, more opaque edge. It's crucial to maintain pressure on the CelPad beyond the edge of the strip to achieve the translucent quality of the frill. Occasional tears and little holes are not uncommon and are not a bad thing! Think of them as opportunities for more light to pass through! Set the frill aside to dry slightly (up to 3 minutes) before applying it to the cake. Use this time to frill some more strips.

7 Use a paintbrush to apply a small amount of water to the base (the unfrilled edge) of a strip.

8 Place the first strip so that the frilled edge hangs over the top of the inverted cake. This creates a beautiful collar effect once the cake is turned upright.

9   Moisten a second strip and place it next to the first one so that it overlaps the first by about ½ inch. Repeat, making your way around the tier until you have completed the first row.

10 Apply a second row of frilled strips: Place the moistened band of the strip so that it rests about ¼ inch above the edge of the first row. Continue adding rows to cover the rest of the cake. Allow the cake to dry upside down for at least 1 hour before inverting it; this helps the frills keep their shape. Drying time will depend on the size of the cake tier and the humidity in the room; the larger the cake tier and the more humid the room, the more upside-down time is required. Err on the side of more time; you don't want to have to reinvert the cake if the frills start to fall too much.

11 This step is optional. Use the Dresden tool to (very!) gently encourage the frills to open. If you are concerned that the frills are still a bit soft or the humidity in the room is high, skip this step. The rows will open slightly on their own. Sometimes the upside-down treatment of the cake causes the fondant at the base to sneak up a tiny bit and expose some of the cake board. It usually settles back down once the cake is upright. If it doesn't, a narrow band of frills can be applied at the base of the tier after the tiers are stacked.

12 Stack the cake tiers and add any finishing touches such as sugar flowers or other decorative details.

DAHLIA FRILL

l flower like fireworks and shimmering sparks fly.

Dahlias, particularly the large 'Café au Lait' variety, have become an increasingly popular choice for wedding flowers, and one I love to feature on a cake. There are spectacular growers in my region, and I am always blown away by these flowers' size and beauty. Here I used gentle shades of complementary colors for the cake, and the natural geometry of the flower repeats the rhythm of the gold appliqué accents.

To support this larger-than-life version, the middle tier of the cake is made out of Styrofoam since the placement and weight of the flower would tear through a real cake in no time. The faux tier acts like a vase, keeping the flower intact (and your nerves in check).

The bottom tier features blue-green frills in a very slight ombré pattern. Make the frills following the same procedure as described on pages 67 to 71, but use a CelPin rather than a Dresden tool for the frilling; the result is a softer wave rather than a tighter crimp. The tops of the tiers are covered in gold leaf, applied after brushing the fondant with a little water. Fondant snowflakes brushed in gold luster dust are placed here and there and adhered with a tiny bit of piping gel.

Instructions for a standard dahlia begin on page 238, but to modify them for this spectacular 'Café au Lait' version, use Gerbera daisy and sunflower cutters for the main flower, adding individual wired petals (cut freehand with a pizza cutter) for extra size and drama. Keep the wires long (cut into thirds) so the stem is strong and stable enough to support the finished flower when inserted into the cake. Once inserted, use jewelry pliers on the stem to angle the flower head so it faces directly out from the cake.

SPECIAL TOOLS: *Gold leaf sheets* ✦ *First Impressions snowflakes set mold* ✦ *Sunflower Sugar Art Gerbera daisy* ✦ *sunflower cutter sets*

MOTTLED FRILLS

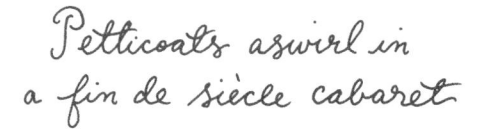

Petticoats aswirl in a fin de siècle cabaret

Bold and painterly frills with dramatic, mottled hues are a fantastic exercise in creativity. Combining distinct and unexpected colors in a variety of patterns takes delicate frills in a surprising new direction. A sleek white tier gives a calm jumping-off point for the spectacular wafer paper flourish.

Start by choosing a palette—here, charcoal, royal blue, raspberry, apricot, and dusty violet, plus shade variations of each. Choose a base color for the first small section; I used charcoal as the background with supporting colors of blue and raspberry. Pat down a small square of the base color by hand until it is the thickness of a pie crust, then press little pieces of the supporting colors into the square. Use a pasta roller to roll the square to a thinness of level 6. It's best to start with small amounts at a time until you are pleased with how your colors are coming through. Longer, thinner bits of color will yield a streakier look, while rounder and thicker pieces will have more of a color-block effect. Cut medium-wide strips of the marbled fondant and use a medium CelPin to soften and thin the edges slightly. Apply them to the inverted fondant-covered tier as described on page 69, gathering the strips slightly as you apply them to create volume. As you move around the tier, choose another background color with different supporting colors for each new section.

Wafer paper forms the dramatic yet very lightweight abstract arrangement on the top tier. Brush wafer paper sheets in petal dust with similar hues to the mottled frills and cut out different-size shapes that are tapered at the tip and wider at the bottom. Steam each piece of the wafer paper (see page 40) to soften it slightly, then gently shape it so it curves and attach it to a dry rose cone (see page 231) with piping gel. Use cones mounted on floral wires of different lengths to allow for dynamic height variation, and make about five individual "flowers" with two or three shapes per flower.

YELLOW ROSETTES

Sunshine blooms...
sweet as honey

Rosettes are as at home on a distressed wooden table in a tent as they are on a silver pedestal in a grand ballroom. Despite having the same core technique as the frills on page 67, they look dramatically different, and the color and composition options are endless. Here a honeycomb pattern, made by pressing an impression mat onto the freshly covered fondant tiers, complements rosettes in ombré shades of yellow.

Working with a small amount of fondant at a time, roll the fondant through a pasta roller and cut it into strips about 10 inches in length, ½ inch at the widest end and tapering to a point at the other. Frill them using a Dresden tool on a CelPad as shown on page 69. Once frilled, remove the strip from the pad and dot piping gel on the unfrilled edge along the entire length of the strip, leaving a little space between dots. Beginning at the pointed end, roll each strip gently to form a rosette. Let it dry for a few minutes to make handling a bit easier. Apply the rosettes to the fondant-covered cake with piping gel, starting from the bottom and working upward so that the lower rosettes support each subsequent row.

SPECIAL TOOLS: *Makin's Clay texture sheets set C*

RIBBON-WRAPPED WATERCOLOR

Elegance wrapped in ethereal painted ribbons

After making countless tiers covered with ruffled frills, I developed this sleeker and decidedly less girlish variation using fondant strips that aren't frilled at all. This ribbon wrap technique is fast and easy and lends itself beautifully to further embellishments, such as the watercolor painting shown here (this design could just as easily fall within the painted category beginning on page 184) and an arrangement of ranunculi and forget-me-nots in similar hues.

With the cake tier inverted as shown on page 66, roll and cut strips of fondant, stopping short of frilling the strips. Attach each strip to the cake, applying a small amount of water to the base of the strip as well as on both ends; this will help the ribbons stay upright on the cake rather than opening slightly as they do with traditional frills. Continue, overlapping the ribbons slightly, to cover the rest of the tier. Allow to dry upside down for at least 1 hour before turning upright. As with other frilled cakes, the larger the tier, the more drying time is required. Assemble the cake with the desired number of tiers, and be sure the ribbons are dry to the touch before painting.

Add a few drops of vodka to petal dust to create edible paint. Use sea sponges or paper towels to apply blots of color. The effect gets better and richer with overlapping, layered color. I find that with abstract painting, the more thought I give to the pattern or design, the worse it gets! Be advised, though, that because the cake's surface is not perfectly smooth, it's difficult to "erase" mistakes completely. You can use plain vodka to remove some of the paint, and the face of the ribbon will be clean, but color may remain in the folds of the ribbon. Instead of trying to be too precise, make peace with the organic nature of this painting technique!

SPECIAL TOOLS: *Sea sponges (such as The Natural Faux Artist Sea Sponge, available from Amazon)*

FLORAL APPLIQUÉ

I love sugar flowers. Quite passionately. I'm always

looking for ways to have more of them on my cakes. Floral

appliqués allow me to have my flowers and eat them, too!

Made with fondant and without a wire in sight, these

lovely decorative elements are both versatile and faster to

make than the gum paste versions beginning on page 224.

JEWEL-TONED
Blossoms

SMOOTH CHOCOLATE FONDANT BEAUTIFULLY offsets richly colored hydrangea blossoms that glint with gold, but you could use any color flowers and fondant. The placement is intentionally random, as though the flowers were carried to their resting place on a spring breeze—meaning this design is as forgiving as it is lovely. Any flaws in the fondant can easily be hidden beneath an errant bloom.

glitter flakes

paintbrushes

petal dusts

Dresden tool

flower cutter

veining stick

vodka in dropper bottle

cornstarch

TOOLS

- ◆ 50/50 mix of fondant and gum paste in desired colors (burgundy, fuchsia, lime green, purple)
- ◆ Pasta roller
- ◆ Global Sugar Arts hydrangea flower cutter
- ◆ Zip-top bags
- ◆ Cornstarch in shaker
- ◆ CelPad 2
- ◆ Dresden tool
- ◆ JEM tool #12 (veining stick)
- ◆ Edible petal dusts (hot pink, lavender, gold, red rose)
- ◆ 3 fine-/medium-tip paintbrushes
- ◆ Piping gel in piping bag
- ◆ Fondant-covered cake tier(s), cold and firm
- ◆ Edible glitter flakes
- ◆ Vodka in dropper bottle

piping gel

50/50 mix of fondant and gum paste

1 Use a pasta roller to roll a small amount of fondant in each color to a thinness of level 5. Cut out petal sets using the hydrangea cutter. Place the petal sets in zip-top bags until you're ready to use them. Working with one petal set at a time, dust the fingers of your non-dominant hand with cornstarch and use them to hold a petal set in place on the CelPad. Holding the Dresden tool like a pencil, thin and stretch the petals by brushing outward just beyond the edge of each petal. If you stop prematurely, the petal will cup and have a thick edge; be sure to brush over the edge and onto the CelPad. Repeat with all the petals in the set.

2 Imagine the veining of an actual petal, with subtle lines radiating outward from the center. Starting on one side of the petal, hold the veining stick at an angle with the point toward the center of the blossom. Press down gently and roll. Adjust the placement of the stick to the center of the petal, and repeat pressing and rolling. Move the stick to the final third of the petal and repeat. Repeat with all the petals in the set. Set aside to dry slightly (you don't want it to dry completely) as you repeat steps 1 and 2 with more blossoms.

3 Brush dry petal dust down the center of each petal. Play with color combinations as you like.

4 Dot a tiny bit of piping gel on the back of a blossom and affix it to the fondant-covered cake tier, pressing very gently into the center to encourage slight cupping. If the blossom is too dry, it will want to crack. There's a sweet spot of just dry enough to hold the petals fairly open but not so dry that it looks rigid and flat. Place subsequent petals directly on top of one another or nestled next door. For close quarters, use the Dresden tool to help slide the blossoms into place.

5 Dip a fine-tip paintbrush into piping gel, then into the edible glitter.

6 Applying gentle pressure, roll the glitter off the brush and onto the center of each blossom.

7 Introduce a tiny drop of vodka into the gold dust.

8 Use a fine-tip brush to gild the edge of the petals, and add detail to the center of the blossoms with tiny specks of gold.

ICELANDIC POPPIES & FALLING PETALS

*Time is suspended and
the petals wait patiently*

I think of these poppies as "statement" flowers, so showy and beautiful, the rest of the cake design can take a back seat, with only a few tiny appliqués for extra adornment. Placing petals along the edges of the tiers as well as on the table lends a sense of movement to the still life. Inside, this particular cake happens to be my sister's favorite flavor—carrot (see my recipe on page 54) with cinnamon buttercream.

The flowers are inspired by Icelandic poppies and have a lot in common technique-wise with the open peony. While not botanically correct, a snowflake mold makes for a beautifully detailed flower center (stigma). To start, insert a hooked and taped 22-gauge wire into a small ball of gum paste as shown on page 231. Let dry before attaching a single molded snowflake with a tiny bit of piping gel. The snowflake should cover the ball from view. As when making a peony, add stamens around the center using floral tape. Cut petals using a round cutter and shape them following the instructions for individually wired peony petals on page 246.

For the tumbling petals, use a pasta roller to roll a 50/50 mix of gum paste and fondant to a thinness of level 6. Cut round shapes from the rolled fondant mixture. Soften the edges using a CelPin and use a veining stick (JEM tool #12) to add veins. Allow the petals to dry on scrunched aluminum foil or parchment paper before applying them to the cake with piping gel. I find that there's a sweet spot when the petal is dry enough that it maintains its shape but soft enough that it doesn't crack too readily under a little pressure. This is the best time to apply the petals. To make the tiny appliqué flowers, roll a small amount of fondant or a 50/50 mix of gum paste and fondant to a thinness of level 5 on the pasta roller. Press firmly into a lace mold to add texture, then turn out and use a small blossom cutter to cut out the blossoms. Once dry, rub with petal and luster dust and apply to the cake with a tiny bit of piping gel.

SPECIAL TOOLS: *Century Lace Mold by RVO* ✦ *PME Flower Blossom Plunger Cutter Set of 4 (the six-petal cutter I use is no longer available, but this one will substitute nicely)* ✦ *First Impressions snowflakes mold set*

PETITE PINK BLOSSOMS

Decadent faces glow golden beneath unfurling blossoms

Fantasy dogwood blossoms perch on gilded, sculptural branches for a sense of quiet and movement all at once. Multiple techniques, including floral appliqué, wafer-paper texture, edible cake lace, hand-painting, and sugar flowers come together to create a rich, layered, and opulent cake. The bottom tier is painted in blues and charcoals and purples using petal dusts mixed with vodka. While still wet, small pieces of scrap wafer paper are adhered to the tier to give it texture and then further painted over. The top tier features edible cake lace (see page 41). Once dry, I brushed the cake lace with yellows, creams, and golds.

To make the tiny pink blossoms sprinkled down the sides of the cake, use a pasta roller to roll a soft pink 50/50 mix of fondant and gum paste to a thinness of level 5 and then cut it into flower shapes. Use a Dresden tool to gently thin the petals and create a slight indentation in the center, gently cupping the blossom. Allow a few minutes of drying time before applying to the tiers with a dot of piping gel. Roll a fine-tip brush in a bit of piping gel and then into some sparkle petal dust. Dot the petal dust in the centers to add color and sparkle.

The wired dogwood flowers that branch out from the top of the cake are made following the same technique as for an anemone (page 257): A yellow gum paste center is made with a wafer-paper surround, then a petal set in pink is placed beneath. A couple of 22-gauge wires taped together using white floral tape create a strong yet bendable branch to support the lightweight blooms. Make several branches to create offshoots and vary the arrangement.

SPECIAL TOOLS: *Edible cake lace mix (see page 41)* ✦ *Crystal Candy Bebe silicone lace mat, Crystal Candy Virginia silicone lace mat*

VINTAGE ENAMELED FLORAL APPLIQUÉ

Jewelry box treasures overflowing

My great-aunt Jean embellished her sweater sets with bejeweled brooches and pins, memories of which inspired this cake. With a vintage color palette of pistachio, turquoise, buttercup, and lavender, this design is at once whimsical and sophisticated . . . just like she was.

This cake is packed with little embellishments, including stylized flowers, molded bees, and tiny balls of nonpareils that look like beaded buttons, all nestled together in clusters. I applied them using piping gel in a loose, somewhat random fashion. For this look of overabundance, avoiding symmetry is key.

To make the layered flower appliqués, use a pasta roller to roll a 50/50 mix of fondant and gum paste to a thinness of level 5. Cut out shapes using a small 5-petal rose cutter. Allow two or three petal sets per appliqué. Use a CelPin to very gently thin the petals, keeping the shape intact. Allow to dry for just a minute or so before applying to the cake, one petal set at a time, using piping gel and allowing time for drying between sets. It's a good idea to start the appliqués at the bottom of the tier so that the subsequent sets have something to perch upon and will be less likely to slide. Edge the petals in luster dust once completely dry. Roll small balls of fondant and let dry slightly before rolling in luster dust and nonpareils. Glue these to the centers of the flower sets and intersperse a few more by themselves throughout the arrangement. Rounds of wafer paper are great for filling in gaps and adding movement. Use silicone molds to make bees in the same colors as the flowers and rub them with a little luster dust. A few lightweight wired flowers and buds can also be inserted into the tier; cover the wires in floral tape first.

SPECIAL TOOLS: *PME 5-petal cutter (set of 4)* ✦ *rainbow nonpareils* ✦
First Impressions insects mold ✦ *wafer paper*

PANSY COOKIES

Springtime smiles from within gilded frames

Growing up in New England, the surest sign of spring was my mom planting pansies in the garden. They are such happy-looking flowers and appear in so many bright color combinations. To adorn an otherwise humble flower, I've given it a wreath of gold. To me, they look like delicate Edwardian pressed flowers. Silicone molds lend them their highly detailed shapes, and hand-painting does the rest.

To cover the cookies, use a pasta roller to roll fondant to a thinness of level 4. Cut out fondant disks using the same size cutter as you used for the cookies. Brush water (or, for an extended shelf life, simple syrup) on the back side of a fondant disk. Place the disk on a cookie and then, using your thumb, gently brush the fondant out to the edge.

Because the cookie is a small canvas and we want to keep the fondant-to-cookie ratio in check, I try not to fill the cavity of the molds all the way to the top. This is a good practice when using any silicone mold.

The border pieces are extracted from a floral medallion mold. Rather than filling the entire mold, press longer, narrow pieces of fondant into small sections of the cavity. Once these individual molded bits are extracted, arrange them in the shape of a wreath and affix them to the cookies with a small brush and water. Let them dry completely before painting with gold luster dust mixed with a few drops of vodka. Be especially careful when painting the interior of the border, as mistakes are hard to erase within the details of the molding.

For the pansy, the beautiful mold does most of the work! I prefer to mold them in white fondant and color them with petal dust so I can create any color combination I like. Once extracted from the mold, let the flower dry for at least 1 hour before brushing on color. Many pansies have a distinctly white, tiny center. To keep this ultra-white with all the petal dust flying around, carefully paint the tiniest amount of egg white (make sure it's pasteurized!) onto this area and let dry. The egg white acts as a seal against color.

For most flowers, I'm most comfortable using petal dust and a dry brush technique since the color layers so nicely. It's not uncommon for me to start out with peach and yellow in mind and wind up with burgundy and fuchsia. A small paintbrush with shorter bristles works well for applying the color. Use a black fine-tip edible pen to draw the "whiskers" of the pansy. As the pansy is a bit heavy, use a dab of piping gel to adhere it to the face of the cookie.

SPECIAL TOOLS: *Sunflower Sugar Art pansy mold* ✦ *First Impressions flower medallions 1 mold* ✦ *YummyArt Edible Marker (black)*

TEXTILE

I often refer to my cakes as "canvases,"

but fondant can also take on a more runway-worthy

personality. Like fabric, the medium transforms into

myriad textures ranging from old-fashioned

quilting to haute couture shimmering lace.

FLORAL
Embroidery

CREWEL EMBROIDERY IS BOTH lovely and charmingly humble. I have an antique crewelwork pillow cover that's just scratchy enough to remind me of the hardworking hands that created it a couple centuries ago. A relatively flat mold provides the right depth for some fine textile details, and ranunculi spring out from the top as if released from the design below.

fondant

flower
mold

cornstarch

petal
dusts

TOOLS

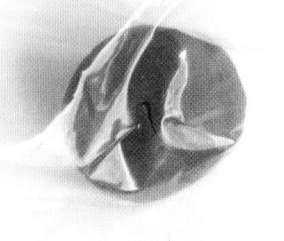

quilting tool

piping gel

paintbrush

craft knife

- Fondant or 50/50 mix of fondant and gum paste (pale pink, medium green, dark green)
- First Impressions flower 2 mold
- Zip-top bag
- Cornstarch in shaker
- PME quilting tool
- Fine-/medium-tip paintbrush
- Petal dust (hot pink, red rose)
- Piping gel in piping bag
- Fondant-covered cake tier(s), cold and firm
- Craft knife such as X-ACTO

1   Press the fondant into the flower mold, with the pink fondant in the flower section and green for the stem and leaves, but blur the connections just a bit. Have a little green encroaching on the base of the flower and add some darker green here and there on the leaves and/or stem. Be careful not to overfill the mold. Keep the remaining fondant in a zip-top bag as you work.

2   Turn the mold over and carefully peel it back, allowing the piece to come out on its own.

3   Continue making molded pieces using selections from the mold, such as a single leaf or a stem and a leaf. Don't extract too many pieces at a time or they will become too dry to place on the cake.

4   Roll the quilting tool wheel along the veins of the leaf and flower to make dotted lines.

5 Use the opposite end of the quilting tool to make little holes here and there.

6 Brush on petal dust as an accent color.

7 Dot a bit of piping gel onto the back of the textile piece. Be careful not to apply the gel too close to the edges of the piece, or it might leach out when the piece is applied to the cake.

8 Affix the full molded piece to the cake, closer to the bottom of the tier in case it slides slightly. The subsequent pieces will be supported by the first pieces you apply. Add selections as you like, working upward from the bottom, making sure that they are connected or nearly connected to one another to create a cohesive pattern.

DAISY CAKES

*Three so dainty
bursting with summer*

I'm always on the hunt for cake stands, and I couldn't resist this sweet little trio. The retro pastel colors reminded me of 1960s prom dresses—lovely, delicate, and snug atop crinoline petticoats. The textile impression on these cakes lends them a slightly quilted, soft look. Darling daisies adorn the designs—perhaps fallen blooms from a handsome corsage?

First, press a texture sheet into a freshly covered fondant tier. It may be helpful to hold a fondant smoother on the top of your cake, applying light pressure, so the cake doesn't slide away from you. I like to methodically press my fingers along the entire sheet to ensure even pressure. This will give you a clear impression. Let the fondant dry for at least an hour before adding tiny dots with fine-tip edible pen, following the pattern of the impression.

Hand-cut leaves and small vines from a green 50/50 mix of fondant and gum paste, and indicate veining using a quilting tool. For the daisies, use a pasta roller to roll a white 50/50 mix of fondant and gum paste to a thinness of level 5. Cut out two sets of petals per daisy. Stack them, staggered, with a dot of piping gel in between and allow them to dry slightly before applying them to the cake. Petal dust can be carefully brushed onto the petals before or after attaching them to the cake. Press a bit of yellow fondant into a mold to create a tiny flower center, edge it in green petal dust, and attach it to the daisy with a dot of piping gel.

SPECIAL TOOLS: *PME quilting tool* ✦ *Alan Tetreault Crystal Flowers*
Shasta daisy cutter set ✦ *First Impressions assorted flower center mold* ✦
Makin's Clay texture sheets set C (lace)

TILE COOKIES

Layers of texture and painting with a rich patina, perfect with Earl Grey

These richly colored, antique tile–like squares are painted and then enhanced with edible cake lace for texture. Cookies are such a great opportunity to try new techniques without the commitment a full cake requires. Plus, a flat, hard surface is tremendously easier to work on than a curved, upright one that is softening under your fingertips.

To make these, start with a blank canvas: Use a pasta roller to roll ivory fondant to a thinness of level 3. Cut squares of the fondant with the same size square cutter you used for the cookies. Brush water (or, for an extended shelf life, simple syrup) on the back side of the fondant. Place the fondant on a cookie and then, using your thumb, gently brush the fondant out to the edges. Let sit until dry to the touch, about 30 minutes. Brush and rub dry petal dust onto the entire surface, layering the colors however you like. Then mix a few drops of vodka with petal dust to make a wet paint and paint a small design, either using fragments of a few different stencils or freehand. Outline the designs with a black fine-tip edible pen. Apply small pieces of edible cake lace (see page 41) with piping gel and then brush them with more color. Last, rub charcoal petal dust around the edge of each cookie to lend them an antique appearance.

SPECIAL TOOLS: *YummyArts Edible Marker (black)* ✦
Edible cake lace mix (see page 41) ✦ *Crystal Candy Bebe silicone lace mat* ✦
Crystal Candy Virginia silicone lace mat

GOLD LEAF
WITH LACE OVERLAY

Glinting in candlelight
beneath dark lace,
Eveningwear? Absolutely.

Gold leaf is almost always the star of a cake—usually presented as a smooth tier meticulously covered in sheets of gold, left unadorned to shine in all its light-catching glory. So how to make gold leaf even more opulent? The surprising answer: Cover it up.

This lace overlay is made from edible silver cake lace (see page 41) shaped in two different molds to give the design variety. There's no concern about the lace tearing or not coming out completely clean. I broke the lace into different pieces, brushed them with charcoal petal dust to create depth and shadow, and then reassembled them on the cake for a pattern that is varied and completely unique.

The pieces are attached to the cake with a thin layer of piping gel. To keep things from getting too serious, I sprinkled rainbow nonpareils into piping-gel-dabbed crevices within the lace. It's as messy and unwieldy as it sounds, so if you do this, a sheet tray beneath the tier is helpful for catching the excess nonpareils. A little gold luster dust tapped onto the nonpareils tones down the rainbow just the right amount.

In keeping with this cake's formal yet free-spirited personality, the floral arrangement on top is romantic and brooding, featuring sugar roses, a garden rose, ranunculus, ripening plums, and deep purple foliage; see pages 224 to 277 for more on how to make these.

SPECIAL TOOLS: *Edible cake lace mix (see page 41)* ✦ *Crystal Candy Bebe silicone lace mat* ✦ *Crystal Candy Virginia silicone lace mat*

FRIDA

"I paint flowers so they will not die".
— Frida Kahlo

This design is a great example of beginning with one inspiration (a Dolce & Gabbana gown) and finishing with another (the work of Frida Kahlo). When I'm struggling to finish a cake, I take it as a sign that it's time to deviate from the original design. The end result is almost always something far more interesting.

This cake is a sea of texture! Incorporating myriad boldly colored textile elements in a loosely geometric pattern allowed me to explore one of my favorite painters in a decidedly tangible manner.

To begin, apply lace-impressed strips of fondant, strands of pearls, and braided rope—all shaped by various textured molds—to the bottom tier of the cake using piping gel. Starting at the base of the cake allows the elements to be supported as you work your way up. Harmonious repetition of the bands of color lends the design a pleasing visual rhythm.

At the heart of the bottom tier, cluster together tiny rosettes (see page 81) with outer petals made of wafer paper around a single wired daffodil. To make this spring flower, tape together three stamens. Cut out a small circle from yellow gum paste and use a Dresden tool to frill the edge of the circle. Slide it up underneath the taped stamens, using a bit of egg white (make sure it's pasteurized) as glue. Allow to dry upside down. Next, make six individually wired petals (follow the instructions for orchid petals on page 251) and allow them to dry. Tape three petals under the frilled center. Finally, add the remaining three petals, positioning them in the "windows" between the previous petals.

To the top tier, apply a layer of edible cake lace brushed with rust-colored dust over the bright yellow fondant. Nestle a single bright pink, closed rose front and center between the tiers. Embellish the rest of the cake in abundance, with flowers, shiny cranberries, sculpted birds, and leaves overflowing from the top tier, and painted brocadelike molded lace medallions here and there for even more dimension.

SPECIAL TOOLS: *First Impressions perfect pearls mold (3, 4, and 5mm)* ✦
RVO century lace mold ✦ *First Impressions rope set mold* ✦
CK Products lace flowers medallion mold

PEARLS

Forget diamonds; pearls are a cake's best friend.
The softly shimmering spheres wrap, perch, or tumble
upon fondant. They can be rolled individually by
hand or shaped into uniform strands in a mold. One of
nature's most fascinating natural phenomena,
pearls appear with abundant variety in both color and
shape. Needless to say, I have more than a little
fun with this technique.

PEARLS &
Ribbons

CONFESSION: I'M A BIG Jane Austen fan, and this design looks like it walked straight out of the latest film adaptation. It wears elegance in a casual, offhand way that is boldly expressive without being obtuse. Why don just one adornment when large round pearls, dainty freshwater pearls, and ribbons are on hand? Pale blue blossoms are an unexpected counterpoint to the abundant arrangement of peach roses, garden roses, and shimmering leaves. How grand!

TOOLS

- 50/50 mix of fondant and gum paste in ivory
- Pasta machine
- Pizza cutter
- Zip-top bags
- Piping gel in piping bag
- Fondant-covered cake tier(s), cold and firm
- White fondant
- Rimmed baking sheet
- Parchment paper or silicone baking mat
- Petal/luster dusts (forget-me-not, blue, gold, rose gold, silver, pearl, lime green)
- Small strainer
- Several small dishes/ cupcake liners
- Wafer paper
- Small oval paper punch
- Silver glitter dust
- 2 fine-/medium-tip paintbrushes
- Turntable
- First Impressions small insect mold (dragonfly)

zip-top bags

petal dusts

paper punch

strainer

insect
mold

piping
gel

paintbrushes

50/50 mix
of fondant
and
gum paste

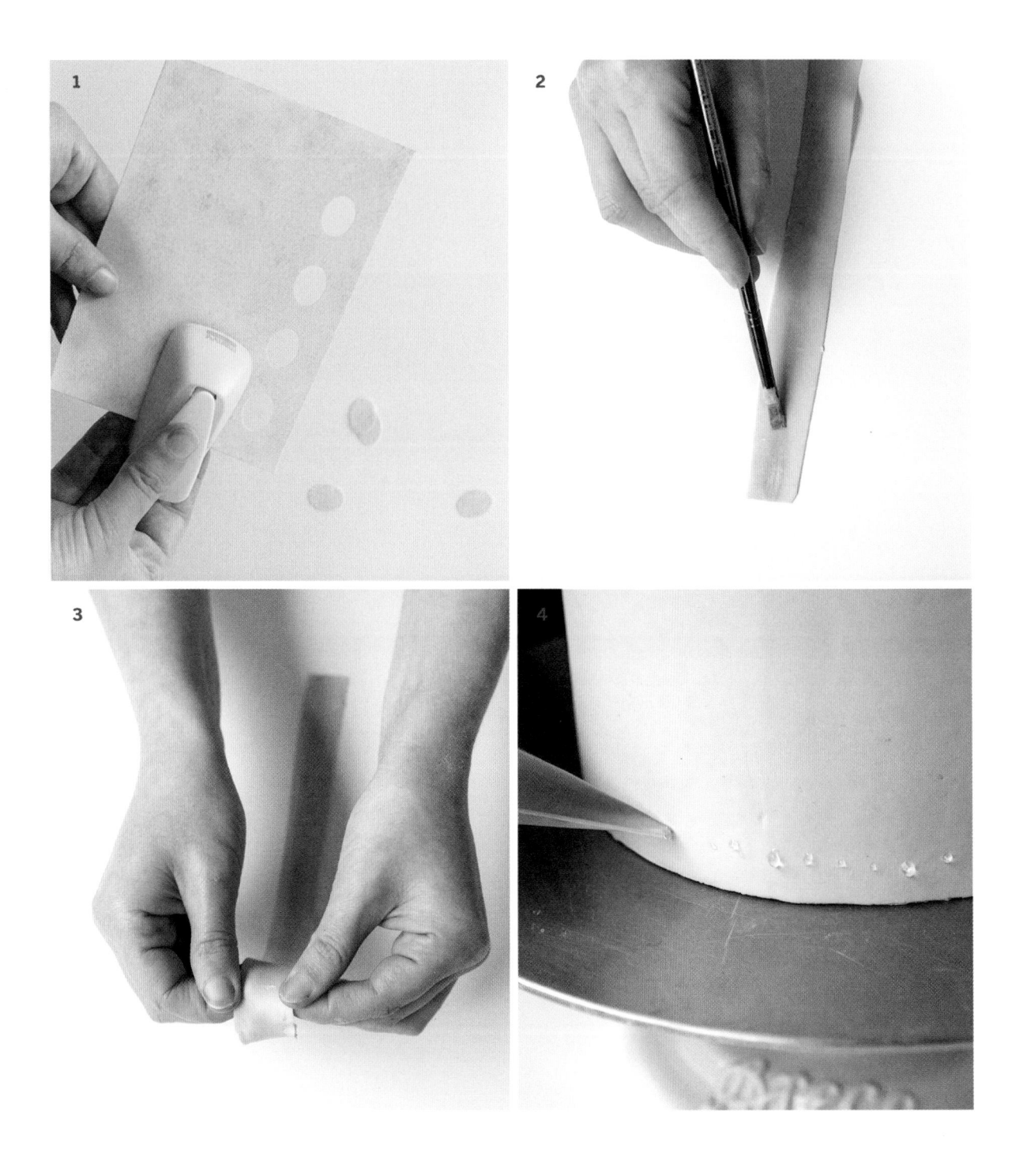

1   Punch out ovals of wafer paper brushed with blue petal dust and set them aside. Press a 50/50 mix of fondant and gum paste into the dragonfly mold. Extract them gently and allow them to dry before brushing them with luster dust. Set aside.

2   Use a pasta roller to roll the ivory fondant–gum paste mix to a thinness of level 6. Cut it into strips about 12 inches long and ¾ inch wide. Brush a mix of blue and silver dust down the center of an ivory strip. Keep the rest of the strips in a zip-top bag while you work.

3   While the strip is still very fresh, use your thumbs to gently soften and curl the sides.

4   Pipe tiny dots of piping gel around one side of the base of the cake tier. Leave a little bit of room between dots.

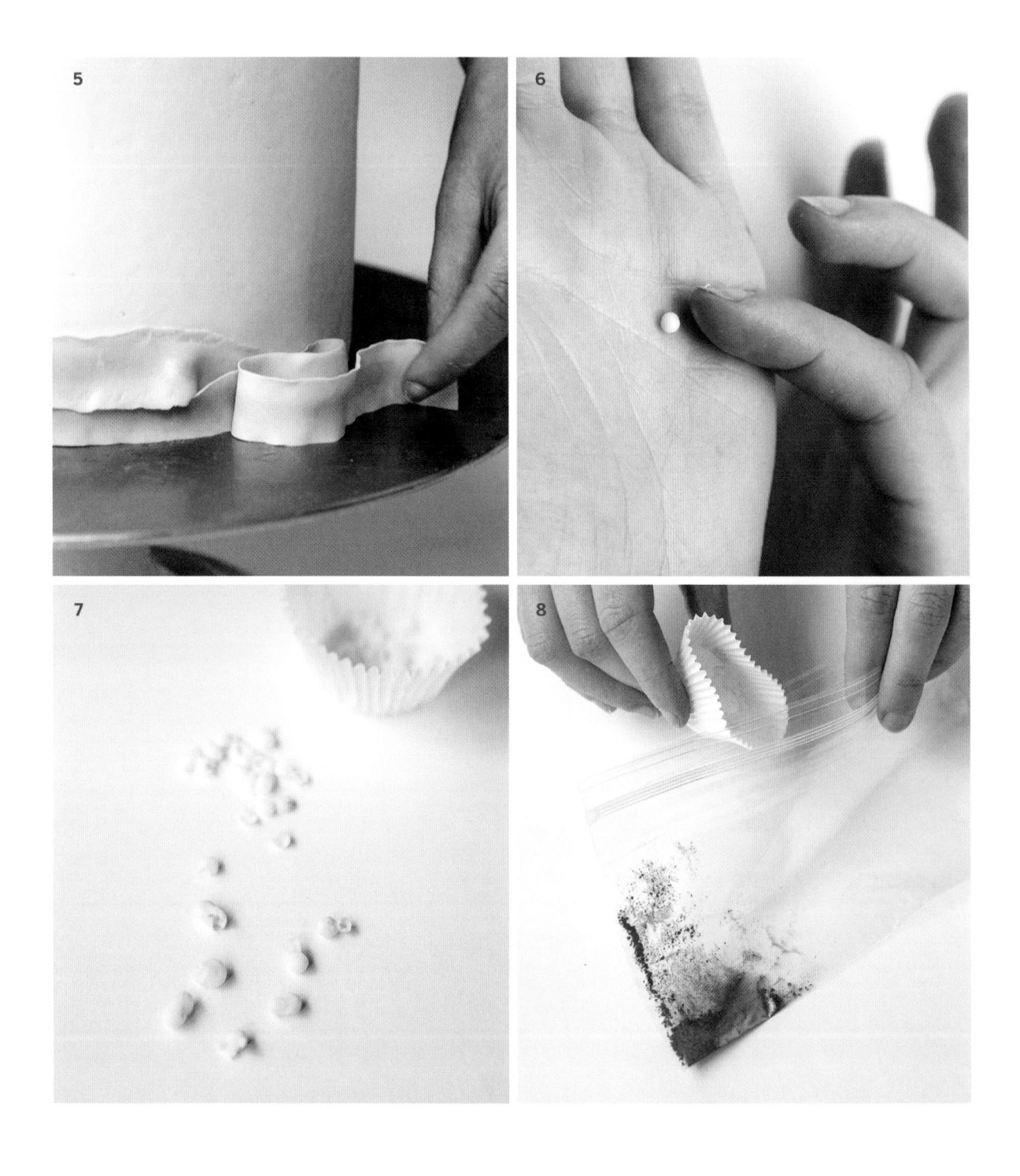

5   Place half of the first ribbon along the dots of piping gel. Leave the other half unattached. Gently fold the unattached part of the strip so that it looks like softly curled ribbon. Use dots of piping gel as needed to secure the folds. Even though you want this to look natural and soft, the ribbon still needs to be securely attached to the cake tier. Repeat with another ribbon, perhaps tucking one end beneath the first ribbon to give the illusion of them being intertwined. I find it too difficult to try to wrap the entire cake in one continuous strip. By breaking it into sections, you have a bit more time and control over the placement. When layering the ribbons, give them the slightest bit of slack so they look draped rather than plastered. Don't worry about seams: There will be plenty of pearls and dragonflies to cover them. I covered the entire bottom tier in ribbons and then used only two or three rows on the upper tiers to leave room for the pearls.

6   Using white fondant, roll pearls of all sizes, from a tiny peppercorn to a blueberry, in the palm of your hand. Set aside to dry slightly.

7   To make freshwater pearls, which have an irregular shape: Preheat the oven to 350°F. Line a rimmed baking sheet with parchment paper or a silicone mat. Continuing with white fondant (be sure it's 100%, not a 50/50 mix), roll super-tiny pearls (even tinier than a peppercorn) and place them on the baking sheet. Allow lots of room between the pearls. Yes, as soon as you pick up the baking sheet they are going to slide around. Yes, it's really annoying! Be sure they are spread out before they get into the oven. Wait about 2 minutes and you'll see your tiny pearls start to grow and bubble. Make sure all the pearls have bubbles before removing them from the oven. They should not be in long enough to take on any color, and the process should take no longer than 5 minutes. Let cool slightly before removing from the baking sheet.

8   Put a bit of green petal dust and a bit of rose gold luster dust in a small zip-top bag. Pour in your baked pearls, seal the bag, and shake vigorously to coat.

9   Pour the contents of the bag into a strainer set over a small dish. Tap out the excess dust and transfer the colored freshwater pearls to a clean container. Using a clean bag and a clean strainer, repeat the shaking process with pearl-colored luster dust and the multisize regular (unbaked) pearls.

10   Have all your decorative elements at the ready: the punched wafer paper, molded dragonflies, green freshwater pearls, traditional pearls, silver glitter dust, and a bit of clear piping gel. Dip a fine-tip paintbrush first in the piping gel, then in the silver dust.

*As the silver glitter dust is for decorative use, you may wish to substitute white edible glitter flakes mixed with silver luster dust.

11   Roll the silver gel mixture off the brush as you drag to form a line on the side of a cake tier. Repeat, returning the brush to the gel and silver dust as needed. Continue working within one small section, applying green freshwater pearls on top of the silver lines in clusters using piping gel as needed.

12   Using the piping gel as glue, add regular pearls, wafer paper ovals arranged in a delicate flower formation, and dragonflies to the sides and top of the cake as you wish.

FOLK ART BEADING

*Bold geometry sets beads
alive with color*

This is as close as I get to planned and orderly—neat rows of pearls in a geometric pattern. Some people might find this reminiscent of a Navajo design; others see a vibrant Maasai influence. When I sat down to work, I didn't have any specific research in front of me, and the design is not completely symmetrical (take a close look!). Instead of counting each individual colored pearl, I let the pattern emerge organically. If clear planning is more your style, you can map out the pattern by marking the fondant lightly using a toothpick to indicate where the colors will change. This design has more than two thousand pearls on the front face alone and is not a project for the faint of heart, short of patience, or low on time. Though the strands of pearls are shaped using a mold and the process is very simple, a small cake will make for a much less daunting experience.

Color several small batches of a 50/50 mix of fondant and gum paste and set them aside in individual zip-top bags. Shape the mix into pearls using a pearl strand mold; I used one with a 4mm cavity, but they come in various sizes. Brush the fondant-covered cake with water in one small section just before applying the desired number of pearls. There is a sweet spot to find when the extracted pearl strand has dried for a couple of minutes. This can be described as "al dente": The strand can be handled without stretching (too soft) or breaking (too hard). Start from the base of the cake to help support each subsequent row and prevent sliding. Work across the horizontal plane as you make your way all the way up; cover the top last. A square cake can feature a different pattern on each face.

SPECIAL TOOLS: *First Impressions perfect pearls mold (3, 4, and 5mm)*

OYSTERS & PEARLS

A maritime bounty, courtesy of most industrious creators

The palest gray fondant, like cool water, floats beneath trailing sculpted seashells, fragments of coral, and open oyster shells spilling their shimmering bounty. These oyster shells, easy to make in silicone molds, are so beautiful! They really are the focus of this cake, so keeping everything else sleek and understated is key. I love keeping some extra pearls to scatter along the table for added drama and movement.

Press the fondant with a woodgrain impression sheet as soon as the cake is covered. Color a 50/50 mix of fondant and gum paste a very pale gray and cut circles using a variety of small round cutters. Round, metal piping tips work really well. Working on a CelPad, use a medium CelPin to give each round a cupped shape. Make a few snips around the exterior of each round and set aside to dry slightly before applying to the cake with piping gel. Allow to dry for at least an hour.

Use your hands to shape round pearls from fondant–gum paste mix; coat the pearls in either super pearl dust or super pearl mixed with a tiny bit of charcoal dust. Red sea coral shaped by a silicone mold gives a pop of color. To make the oyster shells, press neutral-colored gum paste in a silicone mold. Once the shell is extracted from the mold, insert a hooked and taped 20-gauge wire (see page 231). This allows the shell to stand up vertically or perch safely over the edge of the cake. There's no need to connect two shells before inserting; insert each half separately. Dust the interiors of the shells with super pearl dust and the outer shells in greens, blues, and browns so that the interiors really shine.

SPECIAL TOOLS: *Wilton sea life mold* ✦ *Scott Clark Woolley oyster shell mold* ✦
Makin's Clay texture sheet set D (woodgrain)

ASYMMETRICAL PEARLS

Grace reaching skyward, just luminous

My interest in line and form is heavily influenced by my ballet background and is evident in this cake. The design is a subtle gesture, as dynamic and gentle as a perfect arabesque. The cake is also a lesson in balancing excess (so many pearls!) and minimalism (nude tiers!). I've estimated the number of pearls on that single tier to be about 5,020 . . . give or take. When it comes to the structure of the cake, the size difference between tiers is just 2 inches, so even though it looks a bit precarious, the design is stable.

To cover the second-from-the-top tier (or any lower tier) in pearls: Place a cardboard cake round the same size as the top tier on top of the tier to be pearled, aligned to one side. Make pinpricks around the edge. This is your guide for knowing when to stop the pearls, leaving room to place the top tier. I recommend stopping a row or two before your guide so you have a little wiggle room with the top tier. You can always add a strand as needed once the top tier is in place.

Make strands of pearls by pressing a 50/50 mix of fondant and gum paste into a pearl mold. Apply them in rows to the single tier before stacking the cake. Start at the bottom and work your way up so that subsequent pearl strands are supported by the ones beneath and are less likely to slide. Continue arranging strands of pearls on top of the tier until you reach the guide you marked with pin-pricks. Allow the pearled tier to dry to the touch before brushing with pearl luster dust using a large, soft brush for even coverage. Dusting before stacking prevents unwanted shine from getting on the plain, matte tiers above and below.

Once the tiers are stacked, arrange a single row of pearls at the top of the "nude" tiers. To add shine (neatly) to these single rows, mix a few drops of vodka with a bit of pearl dust and then paint it on using a fine-tip paintbrush. Sugar roses, garden roses, leaves, and a single peony adorn the top tier; see the instructions for these beginning on page 224.

SPECIAL TOOLS: *First Impressions perfect pearls mold (3, 4, and 5mm)*

CAMEO BAUBLES

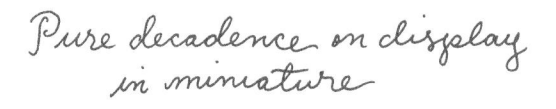

If I were displaying these cookies at a party or reception, I'd have them spilling out of a velvet-lined jewelry box. With a variety of molds, pearls, colors, and opportunities for sparkle, you can create an array of different baubles. Keeping the cookies small means more opportunities to play!

Start by using a pasta roller to roll fondant to a thinness of level 4. Cut it into shapes using the same size cutter as was used for the cookies. Brush water (or simple syrup, for an extended shelf life) on the back side of a fondant shape. Place the shape on the cookie and then, using your thumb, gently brush the fondant out to the edge. Allow to dry before brushing with luster dust, if desired.

Cameos are easy to make using silicone molds: Press white fondant into the deepest part of the cameo mold (the face, hair, clothes, and detail), making sure you can see a clean profile. Then fill the rest of the mold with a different color for the background. Place the cameo on the fondant-covered cookie. Use piping gel or water to attach a few rows of fondant pearls or other molded details around the border. Cookies can be edged in edible glitter flakes; sprinkle them on top of a thin layer of piping gel brushed along the border. Other embellishments include a molded fondant snowflake or medallion for texture and depth, and individual rolled fondant pearls. Brush the finished cookies with dry gold and silver luster dusts, or add a drop of vodka and paint with a fine-tip brush for more control.

SPECIAL TOOLS: *Sunflower Sugar Art assorted snowflakes mold ✦ First Impressions flower medallions 1 mold ✦ First Impressions perfect pearls mold (3, 4, and 5mm) ✦ First Impressions cameo set 1 mold ✦ First Impressions assorted flower medallions set 2 mold*

SCULPTED
FONDANT

I am astonished at the quality and variety of silicone

molds available in the marketplace today. At my studio, I use some

custom molds for specific projects, but I turn to a small handful of

gorgeous store-bought molds over and over again. With such

a simple tool, fondant and gum paste take on a level of detail that is truly

amazing. The sculpting technique is extremely versatile, as the

variations show. From bas-relief molding that takes on the look of carved

stone to hand-painted sculptural elements that are both simple and

absolutely decadent, the creative potential is limitless.

ALABASTER
Bas-Relief

BAS-RELIEF (FRENCH FOR "LOW raised work") is a kind of sculpture with ancient origins, appearing in Egyptian sarcophagi and elaborate friezes in Roman temples and, more recently, American Arts and Crafts–style woodwork. The technique brings subtle dimension to a pattern using light and shadows. Here, the shadows and highlights lend drama to a monochromatic berry motif, and the square tiers are decidedly modern. An ascending arrangement of roses, garden roses, orchids, and leaves, also in matte white, completes the design.

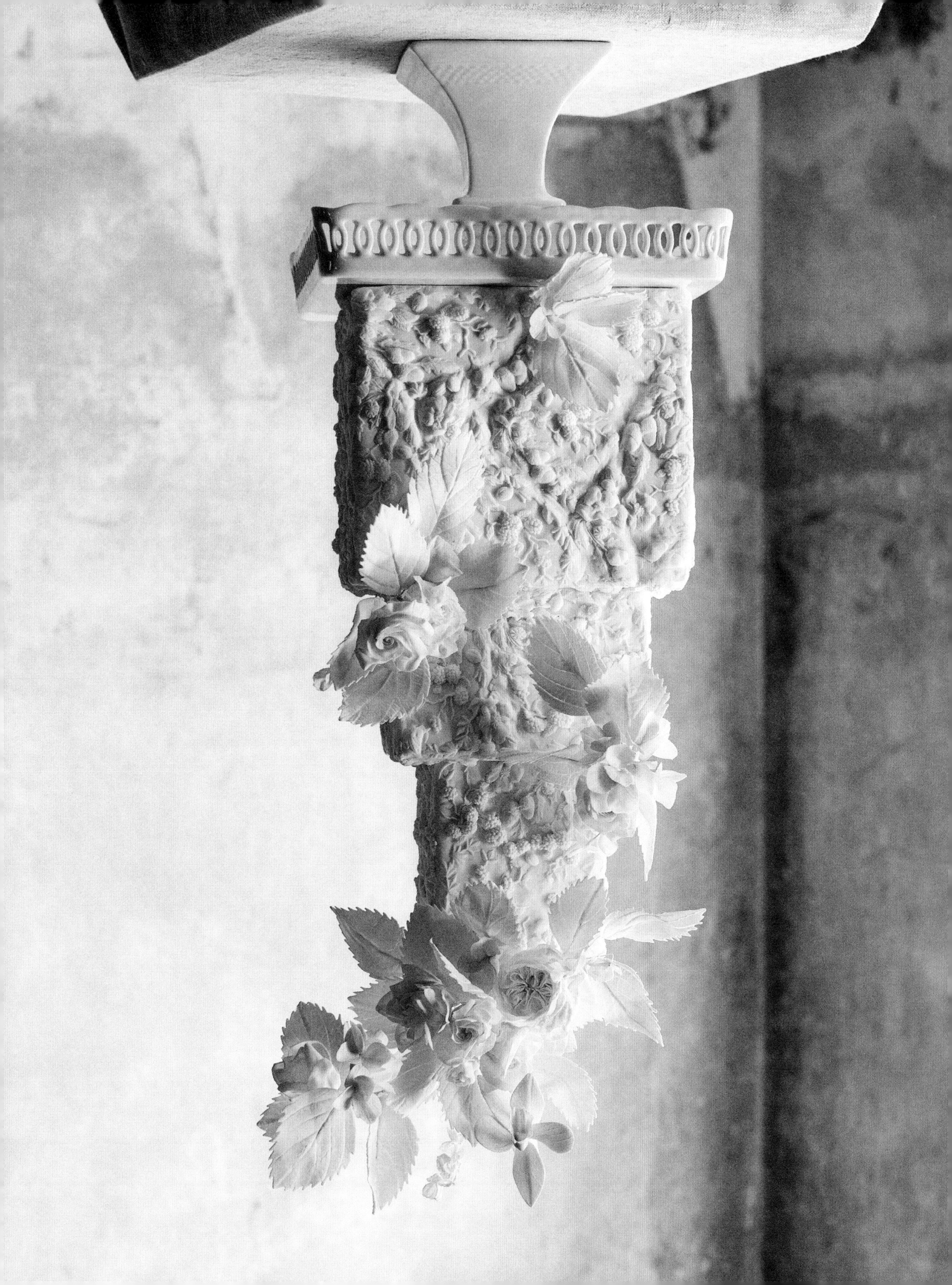

cornstarch

water

silicone mold

TOOLS

- Stephen Benison autumn silicone mold, large
- Vegetable shortening (optional)
- White fondant
- Cornstarch in shaker
- Zip-top bag
- Small paintbrush
- Small dish of water
- Fondant-covered cake tier(s), cold and firm
- Dresden tool
- Paper towel

fondant

Dresden tool

paintbrush

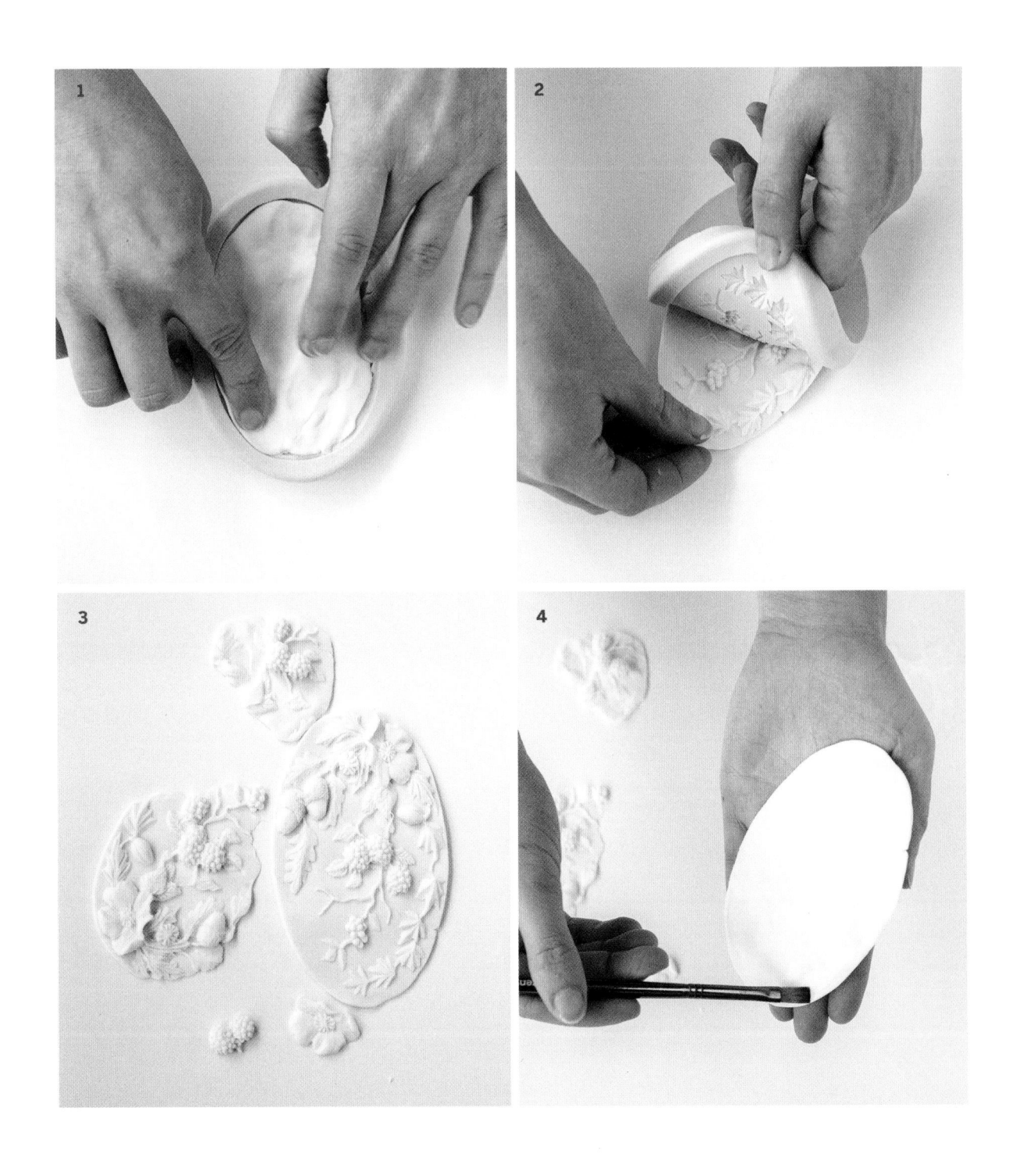

1   If you are using the silicone mold for the first time, season it with a tiny bit of shortening to help prevent sticking. Massage the fondant and warm it with your hands to soften it a bit. Lightly dust your fingertips with cornstarch and press a small amount of fondant into the mold. I like to massage the fondant in my hands first so it is more pliable, and the cornstarch helps prevent the fondant from sticking to your fingers as you work. Be careful not to overfill the mold.

2   Flip the mold over onto your work surface and carefully peel back the mold, allowing the fondant to come out on its own. Do not pull on the fondant or you risk distorting the design.

3   Make a small assortment of pieces before you begin applying them to the cake. Distinct shapes like the berries in this mold, as well as longer, thinner pieces with jagged edges, are great. The fondant pieces need to be fresh for the correct application, so only work with a few pieces at a time and keep the rest of the fondant in a zip-top bag when not in use.

4   Use a paintbrush to brush a small amount of water onto the back side of your largest piece. Keep a paper towel on hand to catch any drips.

5   Place the largest piece on the surface of the cake. Start somewhere toward the base of the tier in case the piece slides a little. This will also help to gently support the subsequent pieces. Use the flatter side of the Dresden tool to gently thin and blend the edge of the molded piece where it will connect to the next section.

6   Repeat with a smaller section of molding, overlapping it ever so slightly with the blurred border of the previous piece. Use the Dresden tool to blend the edges of the pieces together. You can use the tiniest bit of water on the Dresden tool to help the fondant blend more easily. Be very careful not to introduce too much water, though, or the fondant might slide or lose some of its detail.

7   Continue adding a mix of large and small pieces, blending as you go. For the lower tiers (which will have tiers stacked on top), mark a stopping point on the top to maintain a flat surface on which to stack the subsequent tiers. The top tier can be covered completely. If you find you have large "valleys" of plain fondant, adding a small detail like a berry or acorn is an easy fix.

8   Once the cake is fully assembled, use small bits of molded fondant to fill in any gaps between the tiers. Matte white sugar flowers and leaves unify the dramatic monochromatic design.

STONE & HYDRANGEA

A secret garden, lovingly tended

This design is labor intensive, but the petite dimensions of the cake (the bottom tier is only 8 inches square) make it very approachable, much less intimidating than attempting it on a larger cake. If you are nervous about making a square fondant-covered cake with sharp corners and flawless edges, this is the design for you! The gorgeous molding covers all manner of sins, and the soft organic designs contrast with the angular shape of the cake.

Mold the pieces and apply them to the fondant-covered tiers as described beginning on page 167, smoothing the seams with a Dresden tool as necessary. Allow to dry for at least 1 hour before brushing with desired color: For the look of stone, I started with a gray-tinted fondant and brushed it with a mix of cream, charcoal, yellow, and green petal dusts.

The floral embellishment begins with a Styrofoam ball skewered with a hot-glued 18-gauge wire. Clip the wires of sugar hydrangea (see page 260) and ivy leaves (follow the instructions for greenery on page 272 using ivy cutters) very short and insert into the ball. Tape more ivy leaves together to create long tendrils that trail around and down the front of the cake.

SPECIAL TOOLS: *First Impressions assorted flower medallions set 2 mold* ✦ *First Impressions bird trio with nests* ✦ *First Impressions floral medallions set 1 mold*

ELEPHANT CARAVAN

Midnight procession across the stark Sahel

Sometimes the shape of a mold is so spectacular, the best thing to do is let it star and leave the rest of the cake alone. The cake decorating market is pretty vast, and the molds available are increasingly detailed and beautiful. This beauty is custom-made, created from my niece's favorite elephant figurine. If you are adventurous, consider a DIY project using a silicone mold-making kit. Otherwise, you can find a vast assortment of molds at specialty cake-decorating stores.

When using such deep and detailed molds, I find a 50/50 mix of fondant and gum paste works best to capture fine details and extract cleanly. When turning the piece out of the mold, start with the section that is most prone to not coming out cleanly or easily—in this case, the tail. Allow the figure to dry to the touch before brushing it with dry color; I used gray fondant–gum paste mix for the elephants and then brushed them with a mix of brown and charcoal petal dust. If you want the figure to hug the tier, it needs to be attached to the cake while still pliable in order to take the curve without cracking. Attach it with a little bit of piping gel applied to the back side of the figure. For anything "freestanding" (or, in this case, walking away altogether) on the cake stand, or for a figure set on top of the cake tier, use 100% gum paste for extra strength. If setting on top of a cake tier, insert 18-gauge wires into the legs immediately after extracting it from the mold, and let it dry flat for at least 48 hours. Keep the wires long (equal to the height of the cake tier), wrap them with floral tape, and insert them into the cake. Wait until the cake is in its final display location before placing any freestanding elements. Accidents do happen! Delicate pieces like the tail are the most likely casualty. You can repair a broken piece at the last minute with fresh fondant and a tiny dot of piping gel.

The dark fondant background offsets the elephants beautifully. A sliver of a silver moon cut from a simple round of fondant and stars cut freehand from edible silver leaf adorn the dreamy scene.

SPECIAL TOOLS: *Edible silver leaf* ✦ *custom or store-bought mold*

EMERALD TILES

*Primal pulses of
rhythmic energy*

The intricacy of the textures and the architecture of the tiers take what is essentially a green, white, and yellow animal-print cake to regal grounds. Molded peacock feathers radiate from the center in a pleasing geometric rhythm. The top tier features another texture, this time using layered wafer paper. The final embellishment is truly over the top: a jaunty vessel that perches like a festive hat and overflows with anemones and ivy.

Start by making the sculpted pieces, using a green 50/50 mix of fondant and gum paste. Press the mixture into a peacock lace mold. Brush the extracted pieces with petal dusts in green, yellow, turquoise, and gold luster. You can make these pieces ahead of time, but keep them in a sealed zip-top bag so they remain pliable.

Apply them to the front face of the bottom tier with piping gel, overlapping the edges and working from the outside in for the most pleasing and secure placement. For the top tier, brush wafer paper with petal dust in complementary tones (as shown on page 212) and use a craft punch to cut out tiny ovals. Affix the wafer-paper ovals to the sides of the tiers using piping gel, overlapping them to create a shingled pattern. Leave room in the center of the tier in order to place the peacock tiles.

I chose a half sphere of Styrofoam as a unique foundation that's both lightweight and supportive for the sugar flowers. Spear the Styrofoam with a hooked and hot-glued 18-gauge wire, then cover it in wafer paper ovals using the same shingled pattern. Insert white anemones (see page 257) and delicate branches of oval leaves (see page 272) to complete the arrangement.

SPECIAL TOOLS: *RVO lace peacock mold, small*

FLORAL URNS

*A lavish luncheon finale.
Bon appétit!*

It's no secret that I love making sugar flowers. I also really, really love to arrange them. The little molded flower urn on these mini cakes is a nod to arranging on a tiny scale, but with no risk of shattering petals! Instead, tiny fondant flowers are shaped in a silicone mold and then arranged on top of each cake. I used the respective color palettes of these gorgeous antique plates and chargers as a guide for each luxurious floral cake. You can find the cake and Swiss Meringue Buttercream recipes on pages 49 and 56.

Use a pasta roller to roll fondant to a thinness of level 4. Cut rounds using the same cutter used for the cakes. Let the rounds dry perfectly flat until you can handle them without bending (at least 1 hour). Meanwhile, select your flower and leaf colors. Color small amounts of fondant and keep them in a zip-top bag while not in use. Instead of molding one large piece, press fondant into one flower or leaf at a time within the mold, using your desired colored fondant, and then extract it before molding the next piece. Place the extracted pieces in a zip-top bag until you have enough components to make one arrangement. Use a separate mold and neutral-colored fondant to make the urn. Affix the urn to the fondant disk with a bit of piping gel, then attach flowers and leaves in the urn. Allow to dry. Add highlights or shading with complementary colors as needed, either brushing them on dry or adding a few drops of vodka to petal dust and painting with a fine-tip brush for more control and precision.

At this point, the completed disks can be stored in an airtight container until the cakes are fully assembled. Chill the cakes until the buttercream is firm. When it's time to place the disks, the moisture from the buttercream will secure the disks to the cakes.

SPECIAL TOOLS: *Katy Sue Designs pots & urns mold* ✦ *First Impressions flower medallions 1 mold* ✦ *First Impressions assorted flower medallions set 2 mold* ✦ *Sunflower Sugar Art peonies mold*

PAINTING

Fondant is transformed by painted color. There's no wrong
way to approach your canvas, whether with a
fine-tipped brush or just your fingers. Some projects call
for delicacy and precision, while others are bold,
modern, and random. Scale, too, is entirely flexible. This
technique is as effective on a towering tiered cake
as it is on a single cookie.

STAINED
Glass

GROWING UP, WE HAD a Tiffany lamp in our living room. I loved how light gave the pieces of colored glass an almost otherworldly appearance. The organic mottling of the art glass translates easily to this cake design, with petal dust mixed with vodka to make a liquid paint that you dab onto the cake with your fingers, and a simple food marker is a perfect analog to the soldered metal framework. The key here is letting the design take the lead. In an homage to my childhood lamp, molded gum paste dragonflies perch here and there, drawn to the anemones and berries.

petal
dusts

palette

edible pen

vodka in
dropper
bottle

TOOLS

- ◆ Petal dusts (moss, emerald, burgundy, charcoal, dark chocolate brown, yellow rose, golden corn, purple, cream, ocean, forget-me-not blue, baby pink)

- ◆ Palette or washable nonporous work surface

- ◆ Vodka in dropper bottle

- ◆ Paper towels

- ◆ Disposable gloves (optional)

- ◆ Fondant-covered cake tier(s), cold and firm

- ◆ Toothpick (optional)

- ◆ AmeriColor Gourmet Writer edible pen (black; have a few on hand)

1   Tap out small amounts of each color onto your palette. Add a bit of vodka as needed to turn the petal dusts into paint. Wrap your finger with a piece of paper towel and dip it into one of the colors. (If you'd like, you can wear gloves to keep from staining your skin.)

2   If you are working on a specific project that involves a clearly defined flower or scene, you may find it helpful to use a toothpick to lightly prick an outline on the fondant to establish a "map" for your color. It's also fine to let the pattern be random and fairly abstract. To begin, apply paint in one color to a few areas within a section of the tier.

3   Return to the first areas of color and gently add a different color.

4   Continue layering on color as desired. Include sections that have a greater concentration of lighter colors (greens, creams, yellows) and other sections that have more blues, purples, and charcoals. This is where you will start to establish a pattern.

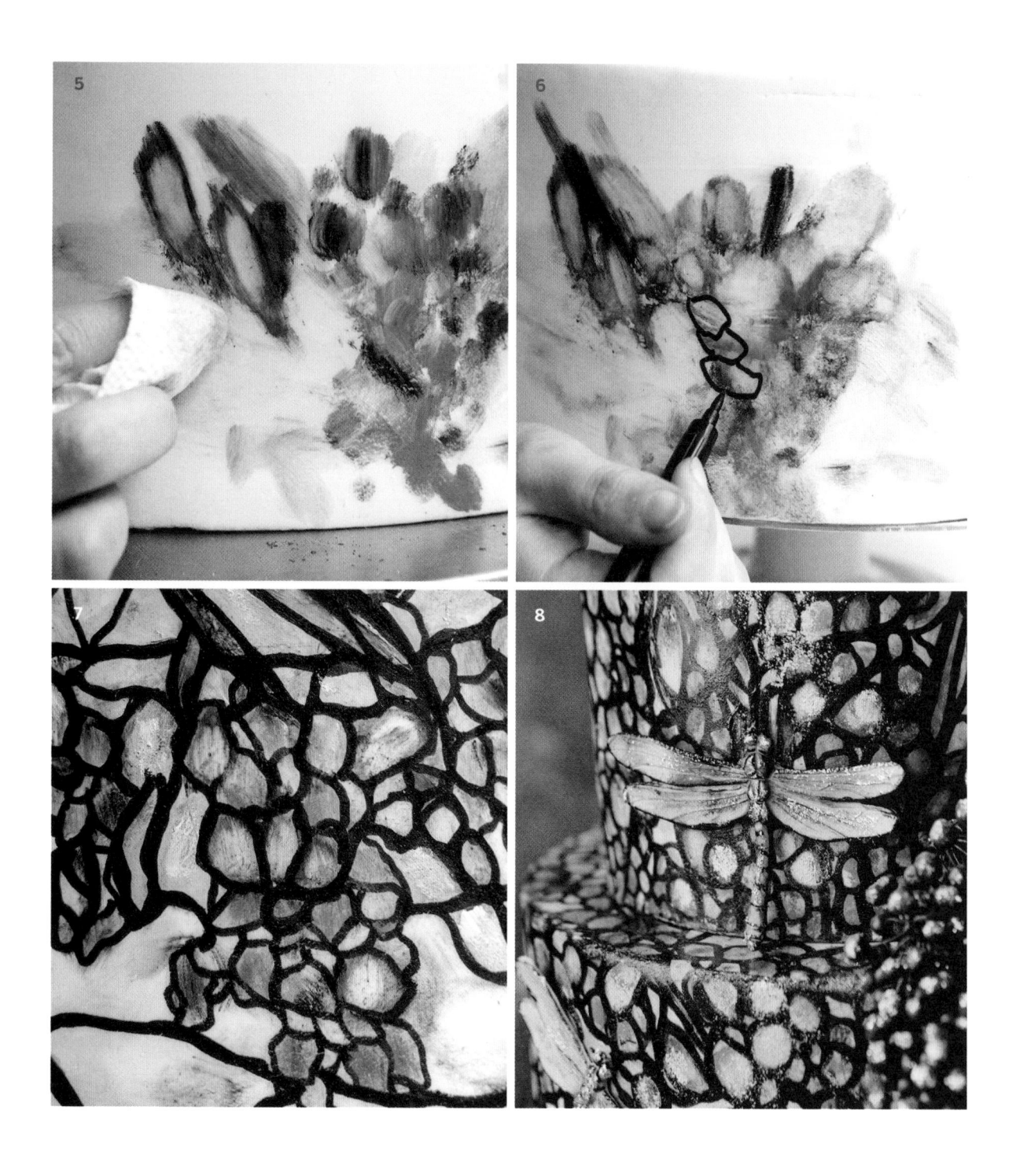

5   With a clean paper towel moistened with vodka, go back into your painting and wipe away some of the color within a shape—as shown in the light-green shapes in this photo. The removal of color is what adds a "lit from within" look to your stained glass. Have plenty of paper towels, both dry and moistened with a bit of vodka, on hand.

6   Let the paint dry to the touch (it'll take just a few minutes) before outlining. I tend to work section by section rather than painting the entire cake first and then outlining everything at once. It helps to break up the very time-consuming process, and allows a freshly painted section to dry while I outline another section. Use an edible marker to trace the shapes you've created during painting. Try to work quickly without thinking too much (easier said than done!). You've done the hard work of painting, so concentrate on simply following your own lead and outlining. Have a few markers on hand to rotate as they lose a sharp point or run low on ink. If you find that the marker isn't working at all, the paint on the cake may be too wet—let it dry before continuing. This process can take a long time if you are working on a large cake. Be sure that your work environment is cool (cold is even better) and dry to keep the cake firm and happy.

7   Continue alternating painting and outlining. If you need to add or remove a bit of color after all of your lines are drawn, do so very carefully and try not to disturb the black outlines, as they smudge easily.

8   I find it easiest to paint each tier separately. As I work, I take note of the emerging "front" of the design. Once the tiers are stacked, you may find that you need to rotate them slightly to bring the entire design together. Like all fondant-covered cakes, it's important to keep the temperature and humidity levels as consistent as possible to prevent "sweating." Once the cake is painted, this is even more important. If you are refrigerating the cake, place it in a cardboard box and seal the box with tape. Before delivery or service, remove the cake from the fridge but keep it sealed in the box. Any condensation that occurs from the change in temperature will happen on the box, rather than on the cake's surface. Wait at least 30 minutes before unboxing.

SQUARE WATERCOLOR

Spare beauty honors
quiet and space

This technique is a variation on the stained-glass painting on page 186. With a softer color palette and a finer outline, it is delicate and refined and unique every time. I still like to use a piece of paper towel as my "brush," but you could use a variety of paintbrushes if you prefer. Set up your palette, then mix your paints and apply them to the cake tiers. Play with overlapping colors with various levels of saturation as well as removing color using vodka as shown on page 192. Allow painted sections to dry completely to the touch before outlining them with a fine-tip edible pen. As with the stained-glass technique, I find that the less I focus on creating specific shapes and patterns, the better. Having a floral pattern in mind and simply outlining the color as it was laid down yields the best results for me.

SPECIAL TOOLS: *YummyArt Edible Ink fine-tip pen (black)*

ABSTRACT "PAINTING"

*In the tradition of Kandinsky's
expressionist paintings, color itself
is given a voice*

This one is for my dad, who (wrongly) insists he's incapable of painting with a brush. Even I often opt for finger painting instead. But this technique eliminates the "paint" altogether, creating a dazzling painterly effect by incorporating streaks of color into the fondant itself. It also brings a lot less mess along with it!

Select a color palette as you would with dusting or traditional painting. For this design, I used bright, bold, beautiful colors, but you could use an earthy color palette instead. Choose a background color and supporting colors; these cakes have an ivory background with navy, cobalt, purple, raspberry, burgundy, lemon-yellow, and turquoise accents. For the background, you will need enough to cover the entire cake tier. Pat out the background fondant into a loose square or round as you would to begin rolling (see page 34 for more information on working with fondant). Working with one color at a time, squish a small amount of colored fondant into the background piece. There is no right way or wrong way to do this. There is not too much or too little. Rolling a thin snake shape and extending it across the background will yield a long, thin streak of color. A thicker, rounder piece will give you a more distinct, saturated splotch. If you lay two snakes next to each other, they will blend a bit when rolled. It will be a surprise whatever you choose!

Roll out the fondant to a thickness of just under $\frac{1}{16}$ inch. If you aren't happy with the result, it's not possible to start over with the same components, as you'll end up mashing together all the colors; instead, you'd have to start over with fresh pieces. Cover your cake and add any finishing touches, such as the gold leaf and sugar flowers shown here. This is a great exercise in pushing your creativity and being at peace with your art.

TEA TIN
CAKES

An heirloom translated and celebrated
(with milk and sugar, please)

Sometimes, inspiration is right in front of me. Literally. This old tea tin has been in my family for as long as I can remember. It lives on my counter and I reach into it every afternoon when it's teatime. One day, I looked as I reached. For the first time, I was struck by its careworn beauty. It had to become cake. It just had to.

Start with square nude mini cakes; for instructions, see page 49. Roll white fondant to a thinness of level 3 on the pasta roller and cut out squares using the same cutter that was used for the cake. Allow the fondant to dry for at least an hour before painting. Add a couple drops of vodka to dry petal dust. Paint the flowers and leaves first, adding or removing color as described for the stained-glass cake on page 186. Allow a few minutes to dry, then outline and add detail using a fine-tip edible pen in black. Use the edible marker for more intense coverage along the edges of the square. Allow a few minutes to dry to the touch. For a distressed look, rub antique gold luster dust along the surface and add some fine black lines and specks using the edible pen. Place the fondant disk on the chilled mini cake; the moisture will soften the fondant as the buttercream comes to temperature.

IMPRESSIONIST COOKIES

Idyllic landscapes unfold on miniature canvases

I'd like to say that an inspirational visit to the National Gallery of Art in Washington, D.C., a 20-minute drive from my house, was the spark for these little pieces of art. That's half true. The other half looks like me sitting at my worktable with my phone in hand, Googling "Impressionist paintings" and squinting at the screen. It's a big effort to get people to actually bite into these painted cookies because they are "too pretty to eat." My advice is to take a picture, and then eat your cookie.

These cookies are decorated by painting wet colors (petal dusts mixed with vodka) on a canvas of white fondant. Use a pasta roller to roll a piece of white fondant to a thinness of level 3. Cut out circles of fondant using the same size cutter you used for the cookies. Brush water (or, for extended shelf life, simple syrup) on the back side of a fondant disk. Place the disk on the cookie and then, using your thumb, gently brush the fondant out to the edge. Let the fondant dry until dry to the touch, about 30 minutes, before painting. Set up your workstation with fine-tip paintbrushes, paper towels, vodka in a dropper bottle, a palette (or nonporous washable work surface) for mixing the paint, and assorted petal dusts.

While I can't instruct on how to paint, I can give you some advice. Avoid using luster dusts, as they won't look as natural as matte colors. Mix vodka into the petal dusts to create a thick mixture: Think acrylic paint with some body rather than loose like a watercolor . . . you'll have more control over the color. Don't be afraid of layering. I often have one design in mind at the start but end up going in another direction at some point. Go with it—don't fight it. Be flexible and patient. You can use vodka and a paper towel as an eraser.

It is possible to steam the cookies to set the color: Hold the cookies by the very edge and carefully wave them through the steam from a tea kettle for just a few seconds until they start to look glossy. Set the cookies on a rack to dry, taking care not to touch the wet surface. (I rarely steam the cookies because I find the matte look of the pigment to be a better fit for the design.) Once you are done painting, let the cookies dry completely (at least 1 hour) before packaging them as desired.

WAFER PAPER

Wafer paper's translucency is so appealing to me. Light passing

through a wafer-paper petal or a row of frills creates

an ethereal glow. It would be hard work to stretch fondant or gum paste to

this extent! With wafer paper, the work is done for you. When

moistened with a little bit of steam, it becomes pliable—and I find shaping

it this way to be downright addictive! It's also featherlight and quite

strong, so there are no concerns about weighing down a cake tier,

and it takes dry color (petal or luster dust) extremely well. These cakes

only scratch the surface of what's possible within this medium.

PAINTED
Petals

NOT QUITE PETALS, NOT quite leaves. These playful flourishes are relatively simple to make—just cut shapes freehand and arrange them in irregular clusters—but have a big visual impact. Changing the colors and shapes will yield dramatically different results, so this technique has no bounds!

wafer paper

piping gel

glitter
& flakes

petal dusts

scissors

TOOLS

- ✦ Soft brush
- ✦ Petal dust (yellow, green, pink, gold)
- ✦ Wafer paper
- ✦ Small scissors
- ✦ YummyArts Edible Marker (black)
- ✦ Vodka in dropper bottle
- ✦ Palette or washable nonporous work surface
- ✦ Two fine-point paintbrushes
- ✦ White edible glitter flakes
- ✦ Fondant-covered cake tier(s), cold and firm
- ✦ Piping gel in piping bag

paintbrushes

↖ *edible marker*

↖ *vodka in dropper bottle*

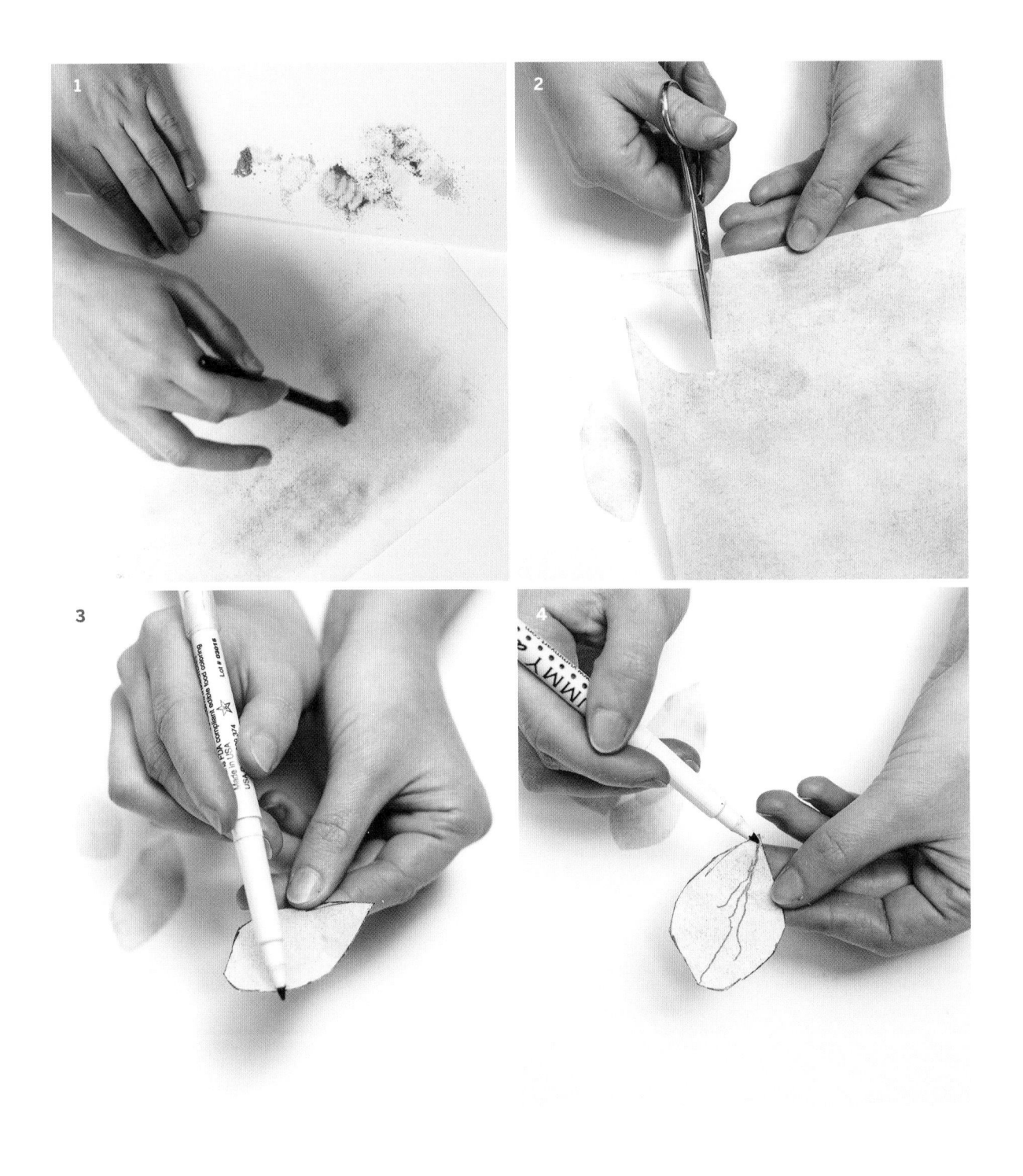

1   Using a soft brush, apply a mixture of dry colors to the wafer paper. Cover both sides of the entire sheet.

2   Cut petal-shaped pieces of various sizes from the sheet.

3   Edge the petal using the side of the edible pen.

4   Draw lines mimicking petal veins.

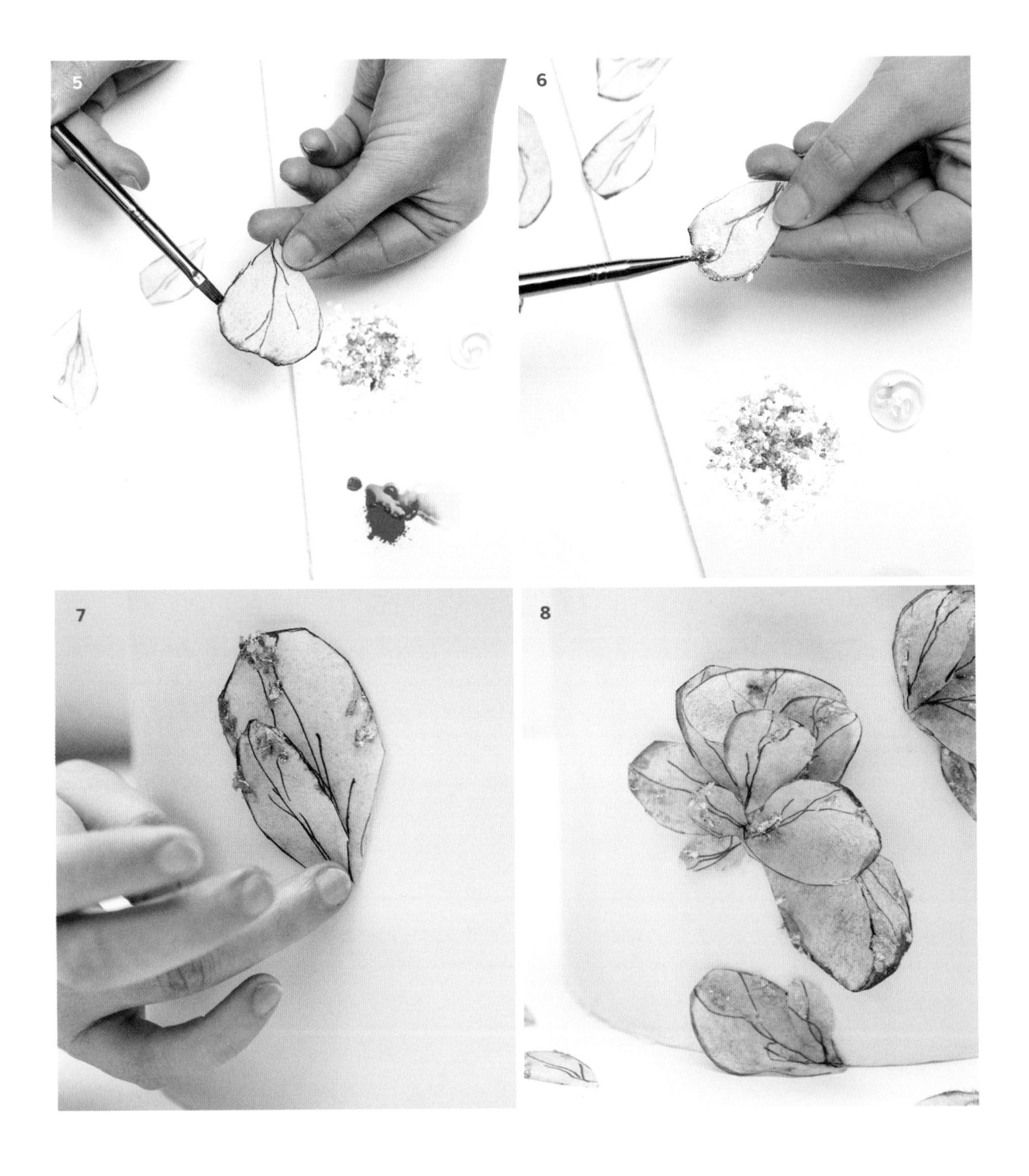

5   On your palette, mix a few drops of vodka with the pink petal dust to form a paint. Using a fine-point paintbrush, edge the petal with color.

6   Mix gold dust into a small pile of white edible glitter. Squeeze a small amount of piping gel onto the palette next to the pile. Dip a clean fine-point paintbrush first into the piping gel and then into the gold-glitter pile and apply the glitter to the edge of the petal.

7   Attach the petals to the cake using a small dab of piping gel on the back of each.

8   Layer the petals freely. If you're using lots of layers, allow some drying time between layers to keep the petals from sliding.

FEATHERS IN MOTION

Operatic drama unfolds its wings . . .

Inspired by Papageno's costume from Mozart's opera *The Magic Flute*, this cake blurs the line between cake and art. It is unbelievably time-consuming, but it's a labor of love. To create a similar effect, brush sheets of wafer paper with solid colors. Use a feather-shaped craft punch to cut out shapes, and group the feathers with their color families. Have a bag of piping gel on hand and a damp cloth to keep your fingers from getting too sticky. Apply the feathers to the cake one at a time, using the piping gel as "glue" and overlapping the feathers slightly as you go. Adjust your angle or switch color families to create patterns and movement. It can be addicting, and it's hard to know when to stop! Be sure to allow drying time between layers of feathers so that the feathers placed directly on your cake tier are completely set and secure before you add more; feathers glued onto other feathers, extending off the cake, will be more precarious.

The "tail" is created by taking advantage of the rigid nature of layered wafer paper. Each row is built upon the previous one. The dramatic extension of the wafer paper from the bottom edge of the cake demands a specific type of cake stand. The one pictured on page 214 is exactly the same diameter as the bottom tier and tall enough to complement the height of the design.

SPECIAL TOOLS: *Fiskars Teresa Collins feather squeeze punch*

FLOWER PETAL CASCADE

A study in contrast—soft pink flowers tumble upon a backdrop of midnight

I love surprising clients with the revelation that any kind of cake—even a pale vanilla bean cake with raspberry preserves—can be enclosed in a beautifully sleek and dramatic black fondant exterior. Wafer paper is so lightweight, it makes large petals look effortless and natural even as they cling to the base of a flower at a seemingly precarious angle. This cake, with just a few blooms, is a great way to begin exploring flowers made from wafer paper. I find the most challenging part is forming the innermost petals. So the cheat here is to start with the beginning of a gum paste flower, such as a rose (see page 232), with just a few petal sets. Brush wafer paper with pink and cream dusts, brushing more color in some areas, less in others. With scissors, cut various sizes of petal shapes. Hold the petal under steam to soften it and gently let the edges curl and cup. Pull away from the steam and let dry. These are the loose petals that can be placed directly on the cake with piping gel or laid on the pedestal stand or table. For flowers, steam one petal at a time and then place it immediately on your tightly formed, fully dry gum paste rose using a good amount of piping gel. It's important that the petal is still soft from the steam as you work. This is not the neatest or most graceful process, and it takes a bit of patience, but you'll get the hang of it! Allow the flowers to dry completely before inserting into the cake.

PURPLE OMBRÉ MINI CAKES

Modern, whimsical, and simply sophisticated

These little nude cakes with layered wafer paper ovals are stunning when individually plated. A study in color, the subtle ombré takes on particular drama when displayed in multiples. Because the wafer paper is so thin, light passes through the layers, giving them an almost ethereal quality. Minimalism and movement, all on one beautiful disk.

Use the same size cutter to cut out rounds of cake and fondant: The cakes can be made and assembled a day or two in advance and kept in the fridge; the decorated disks can be made separately and stored in an airtight box for a day or two. Place the disks on the cold cakes and allow them to come to temperature in a closed box or under a cloche to prevent drying out. The bit of moisture from the thin layer of buttercream on the top of the cake will soften the fondant disks perfectly by the time they're ready to eat.

Begin with an ombré palette of fondant and use a pasta roller to roll each color to a thinness of level 3. Cut out rounds of the same diameter as the little cakes and let them dry for about 1 hour. Cut out dozens of wafer-paper ovals using a paper punch. Place some petal dust into three zip-top bags: one with just a bit, the next a bit more, and the last a generous amount. Then divide the ovals among the bags, shake them to coat, and sift off excess dust. Use a little piping gel to adhere the ovals to the fondant disks in a soft, organic pattern. Some can have an abundance of ovals, while other disks may only wear a few.

SPECIAL TOOLS: *Oval craft paper punch*

BUTTERFLY GARDEN

Taking inspiration from the way a butterfly flutters, this cake is brimming with movement and texture. You might be surprised to learn that these are preprinted wafer-paper butterflies, perched on lacy ribbons of wafer paper. The cake decorating goodies on the market can vary in quality, but these are quite beautiful, and further enhanced by dusting with your own colors. Premade butterflies come in different hues, but a pack of blue-purple butterflies can easily be turned into orange-red ones by brushing them with dry petal dust.

To supplement the butterflies, brush plain wafer paper with cream, bronze, and antique gold dusts. Use a detailed paper punch (from a crafting store) to punch designs on the entire sheet. Cut the paper into 1-inch-wide strips that run the entire length of the sheet. Hold each strip under steam to soften it, then gently gather and pleat the paper to make ruffled shapes. Set aside to dry before applying with piping gel to the fondant-covered cake. Other wafer paper punches can be used to add variety in textures. Carefully and gently crease the butterflies to angle the wings and apply them among the punched-paper shapes with piping gel.

SPECIAL TOOLS: *Craft paper punches* ✦ *wafer paper butterflies*

SUGAR
FLOWERS

My favorite! When I was in pastry school, we had about two weeks

of wedding cake instruction, including a few basic gum paste flowers.

We made all the flowers in white. If you finished your flowers

in time, you could go over to the petal dust station and dust your flowers

with beautiful colors. I took home white flowers every day, and

I did not get an A in the class. That experience motivated me to buy some

basic flower-making tools so I could take all the time I needed

and finally get my hands on some color.

- Take your time, be patient, and give yourself a break. Flower work takes a lot of practice.

- Use homemade gum paste (page 39). You will not achieve the same results with a store-bought product.

- Use white floral tape. The other available colors aren't very natural looking, and white tape can be colored easily with a bit of petal dust.

- Unless it's important to you (or your client), let go of botanically correct limitations and boundaries. Just because it doesn't exist in nature doesn't mean it's off-limits to you. That's where artistic license comes into play.

- Use petal dust as an accent, not for a dramatic color change. If you want purple roses, begin with purple gum paste (kneading in gel color). Do not dust white roses heavily with purple dust. Not only will you waste a lot of dust, but the color will never sit evenly within all those petal layers and crevices.

- Tears and holes happen—all the time. Perfection is impossible and not very interesting. Think of these "mistakes" as a chance for light to pass through a petal, creating a more ethereal look.

- Allow for drying time, particularly for the center supports.

- Make peace with breakage as you arrange your flowers. The first couple times a petal shatters, you'll probably gasp. With time, you'll get comfortable with that sound. It's inevitable and part of the process.

- Always make extra—flowers, petals, leaves, branches. Bring them to the venue just in case.

- Be sure to educate your friends or clients about the best thing about sugar flowers: They last forever! People love to hear that they can take something home to save as a memento. Suggest that the flowers be kept away from direct sunlight and under glass to prevent dust and excessive humidity. A bouquet under a glass cloche on a mantel is stunning.

- Plant your spare gum paste flowers in a Styrofoam "garden." This will not only protect them from breakage but also keep them completely visible so you can find them when you need them. I love pulling flowers from the garden that are the exact opposite of what I had intended and finding that they are absolutely right. It's a great exercise in creativity and confidence building.

A modern take on the Dutch Masters: the sugar-flower still life, featuring a multitude of roses and ranunculus.

MAKING

THE CENTER

SUPPORT

I HAVE THREE METHODS for making flowers. One is the blossom style (see the hydrangea instructions on page 260), in which a complete blossom is made all in one piece, using the holes in a CelPad. Another is using a CelBoard (see the orchid instructions on page 250) to wire individual petals that are then taped together. The third is layering sets of petals on a center support (see the rose instructions on page 232). No one will see this center support, so it doesn't have to be particularly lovely. The size of the center support is important, though, as the petals need to wrap appropriately around it. Use a thicker-gauge wire to support larger, heavier flowers. If you have spare time, make a bunch of center supports in various sizes and let them dry in Styrofoam for at least 48 hours. Once dry, they can be removed from the Styrofoam and stored flat. You will thank yourself for making this stockpile! It's pretty frustrating to get the urge to make a rose only to find you need to wait two days for the center to dry. Follow these instructions to make center supports:

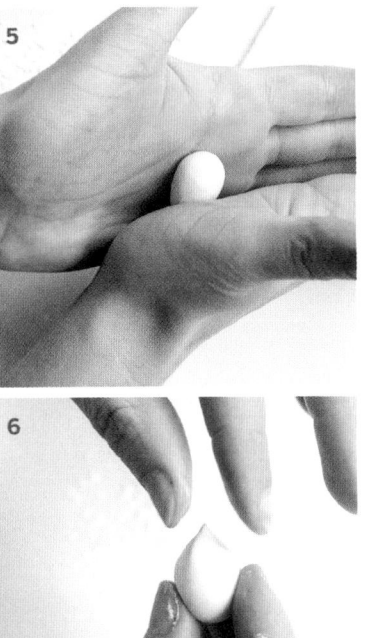

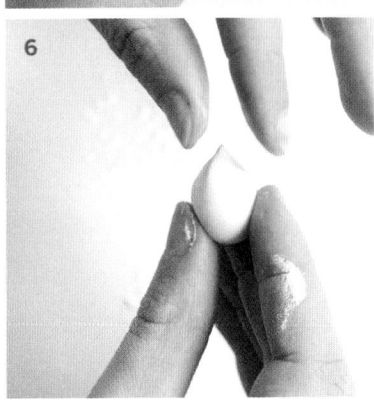

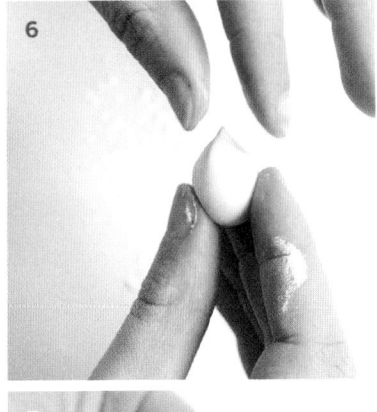

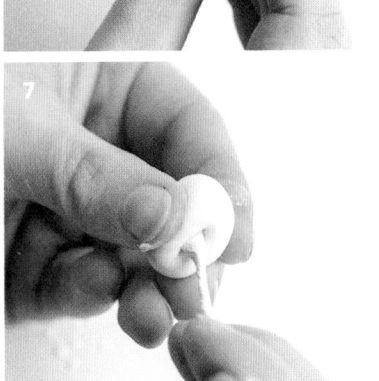

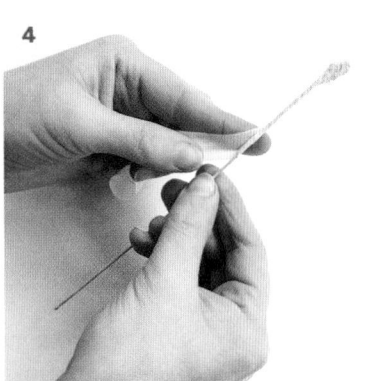

1 Cut an 18- or 20-gauge wire into thirds with wire cutters. Using jewelry pliers, bend a small, closed loop at one end of a wire.

2 Tear a piece of floral tape and stretch it to activate the nontoxic glue.

3 Wrap the floral tape several times around the closed loop of the wire.

4 Continue wrapping, holding the tape at an angle. Make sure the tape stops somewhere between halfway and three-quarters of the way down the wire. Leave the bottom of the wire exposed to prevent the tape from bunching as it goes in and out of the Styrofoam as you build the flower.

5 Condition a small amount of gum paste by rolling it between your hands until it forms a smooth ball. If you are having trouble getting it smooth, you probably aren't putting enough pressure between your palms. Almost think of squishing the gum paste as you roll, and then ease up on the pressure to even out the shape.

6 Shape a gentle point at one end of the ball. This should look a bit like a Hershey's Kiss.

7 Dip just the tip of the hooked and taped wire in a tiny bit of egg white. Insert the wire into the bottom of the cone and push up until you feel the top of the wire close to the top of the cone.

8 With cornstarch on your fingers, pinch the gum paste closed at the base. If you have excess gum paste that forms a tail down the wire, simply pinch it off. Correct the shape of the point at the top as necessary. Place the flower support upright in a block of Styrofoam and let dry for at least 4 hours.

ROSE

TOOLS

- Pasta roller
- Gum paste in desired colors (pink for petals, green for calyx)
- JEM 80mm Easy Rose Cutter
- Zip-top bags
- Cornstarch in shaker

- CelPad 2
- Medium CelPin
- Craft foam square with hole cut in center
- Fine-tip paintbrush
- Egg white in small dish
- Dry rose cone center support built on 18-gauge wire (see page 231)

- Styrofoam block
- Dresden tool
- FMM 70mm calyx cutter
- Spring-action scissors
- Small paintbrushes
- Petal dusts in desired colors

1 Use a pasta roller to roll the pink gum paste to a thinness of level 6. Cut out 3 sets of petals using a rose cutter. Keep all gum paste and petal sets sealed in zip-top bags when not in use. For this rose, I colored the gum paste in several shades of pink (see the instructions for ombré frills on page 67) and will have the most saturated color at the center of the flower, working my way through to the lightest color on the last set. Dust your fingers with cornstarch if your hands are warm and the paste

feels sticky. Place one petal set on a CelPad and hold it firmly in place with your nondominant hand. Hold the CelPin like a pencil at a slight angle and thin the petals by brushing outward over the edge of each petal. Be sure to brush past the edge of the gum paste, continuing onto the CelPad, to make the edge as thin as possible. If you stop prematurely, you will build up the gum paste on the edge of the petals and end up with a cupped effect. Continue thinning all the petals on the set.

2 Lift the petal set onto the center of the craft foam square with a hole cut in the center. Use the paintbrush to apply a little egg white to the center of the petal set. Insert the wire stem of the dry rose cone downward through the center of the petal set through the hole in the center of the board. Establish the order of petals, with petal 1 being at the top position, continuing clockwise with petals 2, 3, 4, and 5. It's important to recall and return to this orientation (with petal 1 at the top) as you build the first layer of the rose. Brush egg white halfway up petal 1 and along either side, stopping just shy of the top of the petal.

3 Lift the petal straight up, wrap one side around the cone, and press firmly. Wrap the other side so that it clearly crosses over and attach. Don't worry about covering the "belly" of the rose cone or about overlapping exactly at the point of the cone; the cone is merely a guide. The overlap of this first petal can happen slightly above the point of the cone. The most important thing is that it truly overlaps. Do not be tempted to simply bring the sides of the petal close together and pinch.

4 Keeping the craft pad in the same orientation, skip petal 2 and move on to petal 3. Brush egg white halfway up the petal and along the right edge only, all the way up to the top.

5   Lift up petal 3 and bring it counterclockwise around the back of the cone. If you imagine the rose cone to have a face, attach the edge of the petal at the rose's left ear. This petal should be ever so slightly taller than petal 1. Leave the other half of the petal (the dry edge) open, like a door. As you work, think of the petals' visible edges as "doors" that open and close; you will slide each new petal into an open door and then close the doors by gently smoothing/shaping the edges.

6   Keeping the craft pad in the same orientation, skip petal 4 and move on to petal 5. Brush egg white halfway up the petal and along the right edge all the way up to the top.

7   Lift petal 5 and place it as far into the open door from petal 3 as possible. Think of attaching this to the back of its head.

8   Once petal 5 is tucked in as far as it can go, gently close the doors of petals 3 and 5, encouraging a spiral. You should see an S shape in the center. Try to keep all the petals slightly taller than petal 1.

9   Brush egg white halfway up petal 2 and along the right edge all the way up to the top. Reopen door 3 slightly to make room for petal 2.

10   Gently encourage the spiral by closing the doors slightly.

11   Brush egg white halfway up petal 4 and just a tiny bit up both sides.

12   This petal is going to sit over the seam created by one side of petal 5. Depending on how much you stretched your petals and how far you tucked the previous petals in toward

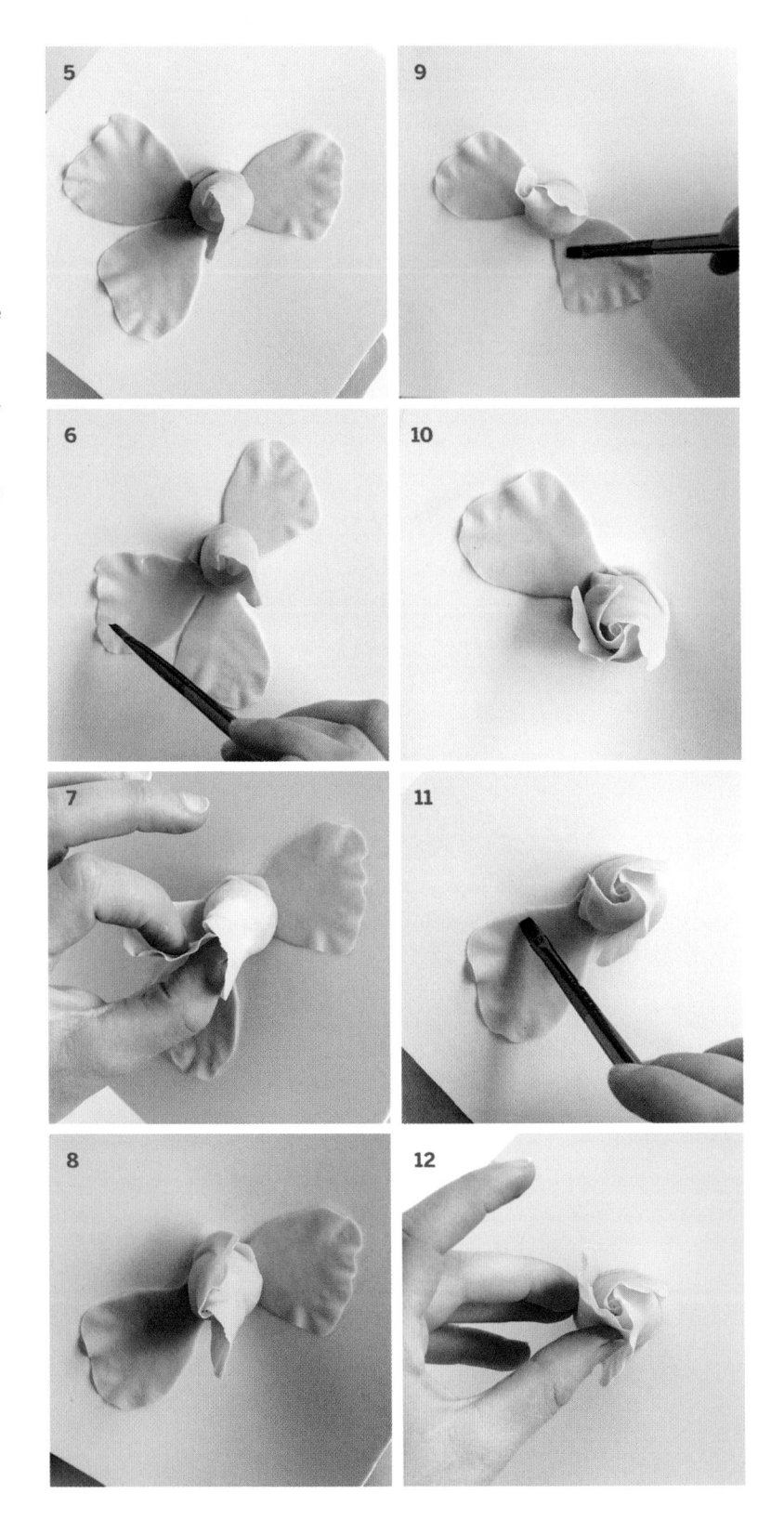

13

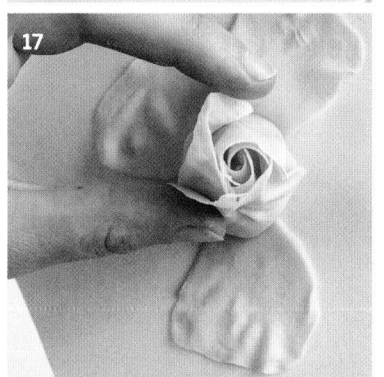

14

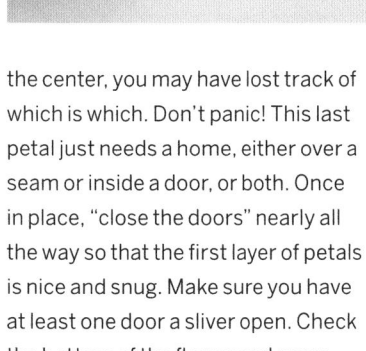

15

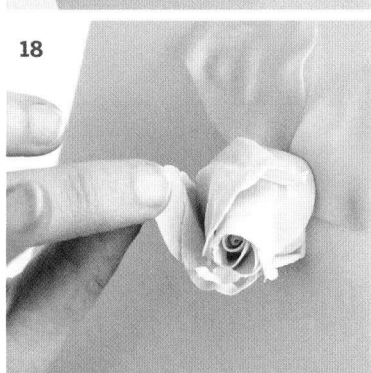

16

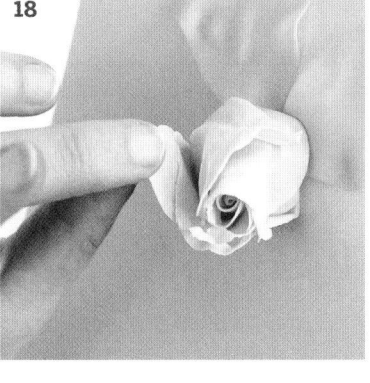

17

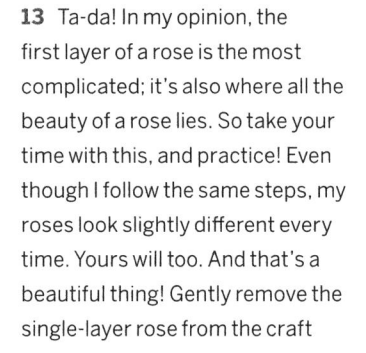

18

the center, you may have lost track of which is which. Don't panic! This last petal just needs a home, either over a seam or inside a door, or both. Once in place, "close the doors" nearly all the way so that the first layer of petals is nice and snug. Make sure you have at least one door a sliver open. Check the bottom of the flower and press out any large seams.

13 Ta-da! In my opinion, the first layer of a rose is the most complicated; it's also where all the beauty of a rose lies. So take your time with this, and practice! Even though I follow the same steps, my roses look slightly different every time. Yours will too. And that's a beautiful thing! Gently remove the single-layer rose from the craft

foam square. Insert the stem into a Styrofoam block and let the first layer dry for at least 15 minutes before adding the next petal set.

14 Repeat step 1 with the second petal set. Place the thinned petal set on the craft pad. Brush egg white in the center and insert the single-layer rose. Good news! This time there is no counting of petals, and no hard and fast rules to follow! Look for an open door as a place to start, and alternate petals as you work. Always brush the petal with egg white about halfway up and then nearly all the way up on the right edge only. This will help you keep the spiral going in the right direction. So pick a petal to start with and brush with egg white.

15 Slide the edge of the first petal into an open door of your choice and secure it as far in as you can. Try to keep this entire set of petals as tall as the first set and keep the petals fairly closed to continue the spiral.

16 Pull the petal gently on the left to stretch, leaving the left edge slightly open.

17 Moving clockwise, skip a petal and apply egg white to the next one, halfway up and on the right edge. Open the previous petal door slightly, slide this one in as close as you can, and then gently press the previous petal to close the door.

18 Return to the skipped petal and brush egg white halfway up and just a bit on both sides. Lift straight up and place the petal so that it follows the curve of the spiral.

19 Open the previous door slightly, apply egg white to the second-to-last petal, and slide it into the open door.

20 Find a home for the last petal on this second layer of your rose. Make sure the petals are still nice and snug. Carefully remove the rose from the craft foam. Insert the stem into the Styrofoam and let dry for at least 15 minutes before applying another layer.

21 Repeat step 1. This third layer (and any subsequent layers you may want to add) gets an additional treatment. Hold a Dresden tool like a pencil and place the flatter side just before the petal edge. Apply a bit of pressure as you make gently pulling motions, moving parallel to the petal edge. The petal should curl. If it doesn't, you might not be putting enough pressure on the petal, the petal is too dry, or you've thinned the petal so much with the CelPin that there is not enough paste left to curl. Continue curling all the petals in the set.

22 Lay the petal set upside down on the craft foam square. The petals should be curling down toward the foam. Brush the center with egg white and insert the rose.

23 Follow steps 15–20 to arrange the third layer of petals in the same way as the second layer. The only difference when applying this third set is the height of the brushed egg white. Because you want to give the appearance that the rose is starting to open, brush egg white only halfway up each petal and a tiny bit higher on the right edge. Use your judgment. If the petal is falling backward, add

a dab of egg white to hold it in place. Continue attaching the petals on the right and leaving the left side ever so slightly open. Gently remove the rose from the craft foam. Insert the stem end into the Styrofoam and let dry for at least 15 minutes before attaching the calyx.

24 Use the pasta roller to roll green gum paste to a thinness of level 6. Cut out the calyx with the cutter. Use the Dresden tool to thin the "legs" of the calyx.

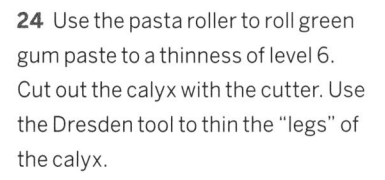

25 Use small spring-action scissors to make little snips into each leg. I like to do one snip down the center and a few off to each side at a steep angle.

26 Set the calyx on the craft foam square. Brush egg white in the center. Insert the rose. Brush egg white about halfway up each leg of the calyx.

27 Lift each leg straight up and attach it to the rose. You can be strategic here and use the legs to cover any unsightly seams you may have from stretched petals. Curl back the snipped sections of the legs to give them some movement.

28 Use a soft brush to tap a complementary color of petal dust into the center of the rose. Touch the brush ever so gently along the outer petals in just a few places to indicate the color from the center of the rose. Brush a bit of green petal dust mixed with a tiny bit of brown onto the calyx and partly down the taped "stem."

DAHLIA

TOOLS

- Pasta roller
- Gum paste in desired color
- JEM 60mm Easy Rose Cutter
- Zip-top bags
- Cornstarch in shaker

- CelPad 2
- Medium CelPin
- Craft foam square with hole cut in center
- 2 fine-tip paintbrushes
- Egg white in small dish

- Dry rose cone center support built on 18-gauge wire (see page 231)
- Styrofoam block
- Vodka in dropper bottle
- Gold luster dust

2 Transfer the petal set to the craft foam square. Use a fine-tip paintbrush to brush egg white on either side of a petal, just about halfway up. Repeat with the other petals.

3 Fold one side of a petal toward the center. Then fold the other side so that it overlaps the first side. Repeat with the other petals.

4 Brush the center of the petal set with egg white. Insert the wire stem of the dry rose cone downward through the center of the petal set through the hole in the center of the board. Brush the base of each folded petal with egg white up to the opening.

5 Bring all five petals close together over the rose cone, making sure that no part of the cone is visible. Gently remove the single-layer dahlia from the craft foam. Bend the wire and insert the stem close to the edge of a Styrofoam block so the flower hangs upside down and let dry for at least 1 hour before continuing with additional layers. It's important to allow plenty of drying time to ensure this first layer stays closed, since it is prone to opening when the subsequent layers are added. If you can leave it overnight, that's even better.

6 Thin the edges of the second petal set as described in step 1, then repeat steps 2–3. Stop just short of brushing each folded petal with egg white. Instead, thin and shape another petal set. Return to the folded petal set on the craft pad. Brush the center with egg white. Carefully lift the second folded petal set and set it on top of the first, staggering the petals. Brush the center and each folded petal (from both sets) with egg white.

1 Use a pasta roller to roll the gum paste to a thinness of level 6. Cut out 11 petal sets with the rose cutter. Keep all gum paste and petal sets in sealed zip-top bags when not in use. Dust your fingers with cornstarch if your hands are warm and the paste feels sticky. Place one petal set on a CelPad and hold it firmly in place with your nondominant hand. Hold the CelPin like a pencil at a slight angle and thin the petals by brushing outward over the edge of each petal. Be sure to brush past the edge of the gum paste, continuing onto the CelPad, to make the edge as thin as possible. If you stop prematurely, you will build up the gum paste on the edge of the petals and end up with a cupped effect. Continue thinning all the petals on the set.

7 Insert the wire stem of the single-layer dahlia through the center of the petal sets on the craft board. Turn the flower upside down and lift off the craft foam. Apply gentle but consistent pressure along the base of the flower to make sure the double petal set adheres well to the single-layer dahlia. Bend the wire and place it back into the Styrofoam to dry for at least 1 hour.

8 Repeat the process, making and attaching 4 more double sets, for a finished petal set count of 11. This technique yields a rounder, fluffier dahlia. Should you want a larger, more spread-out flower, simply increase the petal cutter size every 2 double sets or so.

9 The dahlia, with all its beautiful rounded petals, is a perfect candidate for gold edging. Apply a few drops of vodka to gold luster dust. Flip the flower upside down and paint an indication of a calyx on the underside. Continue down the stem a bit. Use a fine-tip brush to paint the petal edges. Insert the stem into the Styrofoam and let the flower dry, being careful not to touch the wet paint.

GARDEN ROSE

TOOLS

- Pasta roller
- Gum paste in desired colors (medium ivory and pale ivory)
- Zip-top bags
- JEM 60mm Easy Rose Cutter
- Cornstarch in shaker
- CelPad 2
- Medium CelPin
- Dresden tool
- Dry rose cone center support built on 18-gauge wire (see page 231)
- Craft foam square with hole cut in center
- Fine-tip paintbrush
- Egg white in small dish
- JEM 110mm Easy Rose Cutter
- Small paintbrushes
- Petal dusts in desired colors

1 Use a pasta roller to roll medium ivory gum paste to a thinness of level 6. Cut out 6 petal sets with a 60mm rose cutter. Keep all gum paste and petal sets in sealed zip-top bags when not in use. Dust your fingers with cornstarch if your hands are warm and the paste feels sticky. Place one petal set on a CelPad and hold it firmly in place with your nondominant hand. Hold the CelPin like a pencil at a slight angle and thin the petals by brushing outward over the edge of each petal. Be sure to brush past the edge of the gum paste, continuing onto the CelPad, to make the edge as thin as possible. If you stop prematurely, you will build up the gum paste on the edge of the petals and end up with a cupped effect. Continue thinning all the petals on the set.

2 Transfer the petal set to the craft foam square. Use a fine-tipped paintbrush to brush egg white on the center. Insert the wire stem of the dry rose cone downward through the center of the petal set through the hole in the center of the board.

3 Brush egg white along both sides of each petal, about halfway up. Lift the first petal straight up and press it so that it starts to hug the cone slightly.

4 Allow the bottom of the petal to attach to the cone, then pinch together the edges of the top half of the petal and pull back slightly so that the petal is perpendicular to the cone.

5 Continue pinching and applying the rest of the petals, moving them a bit so they are all lined up on one side. Don't worry if a petal disconnects from the petal base. Just be sure it has a good connection to the rose cone. Gently remove from the craft foam. Insert the stem into a block of Styrofoam and let dry for a few minutes while you work on the second petal set.

6 Thin the second set of petals as described in step 1, then repeat steps 2–6, arranging the petals on the opposite side of the first set. Once both sets are in place, fan out the petals just a bit so the gaps are fairly even. Let dry for only a few minutes as you work on the third petal set.

7 Thin the edges of the third petal set, insert the flower, and then apply egg along either side about halfway up. This time, instead of pressing the edges of the petal together, lift up a petal slightly and shape it so that it "hugs" a petal from the first set and sits ever so slightly higher. Continue "hugging" half the petals (the first set). Then repeat again with another petal set and finish shaping them so that they hug the remaining petals (the second set).

8 Gently cup the flower in the palm of one hand and very gently squish and twist the petals to encourage the look of softness and movement. You may need to do this a few times to be sure there is a noticeable twist. Insert the stem into the Styrofoam and let dry slightly while you work on the outer petals.

9 Use a pasta roller to roll pale ivory gum paste to a thinness of level 6. Cut out 4 petal sets using a 110mm rose cutter. Keep the petal sets in a zip-top bag when not in use. Place one petal set on the CelPad. Lift and overlap one petal about two-thirds of the way across the petal next to it.

10 Use the CelPin and a bit of pressure to press down and smooth the seal between the two petals, creating one "super petal."

11 Brace the petal set with your nondominant hand, then thin and stretch the super petal with the CelPin. Repeat with two more petals. The last petal doesn't have a mate, so make sure that you use a lot of strength to stretch him as much as possible. Think of stretching more widthwise than lengthwise.

12 Switch to the Dresden tool and apply lots of pressure just before the edge of each petal, allowing the petal to curl. These outer petals can be challenging because they take a bit more time to prepare, which means they're more likely to dry out as you work, which means a greater risk of tearing or insufficient curling. That's okay! With practice you will get faster. Make sure you are using fresh, soft gum paste conditioned with a little shortening before rolling.

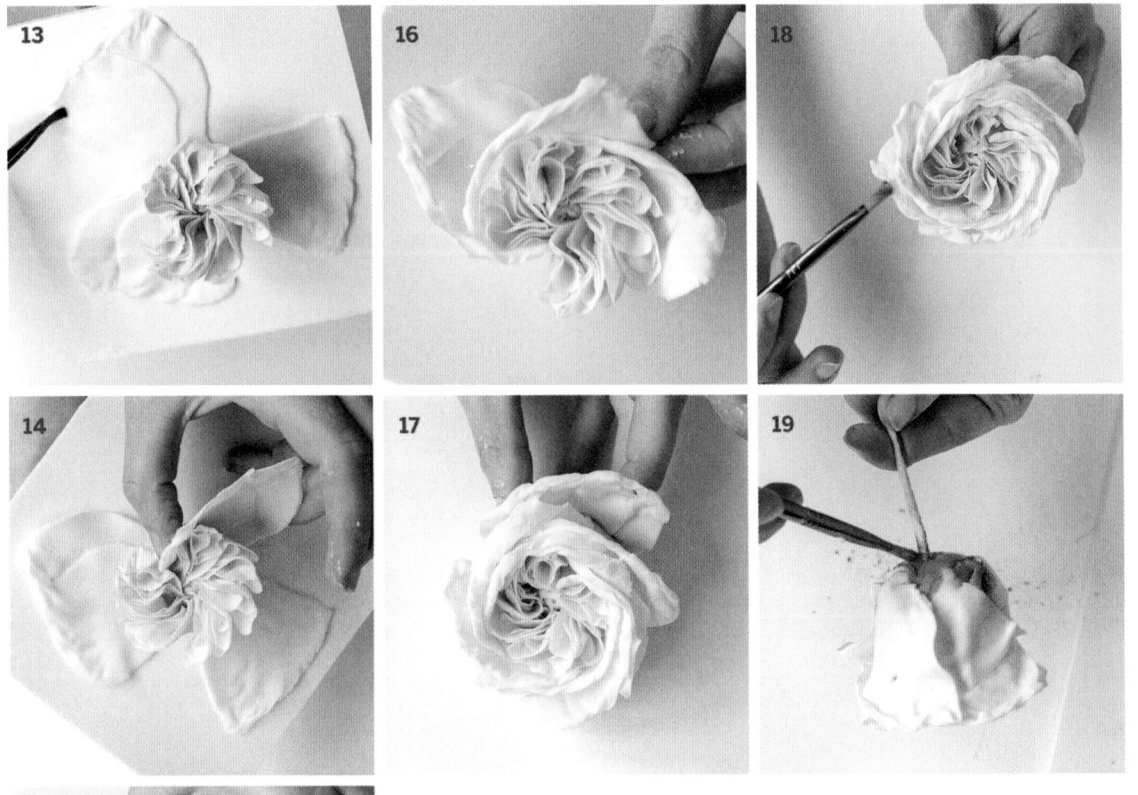

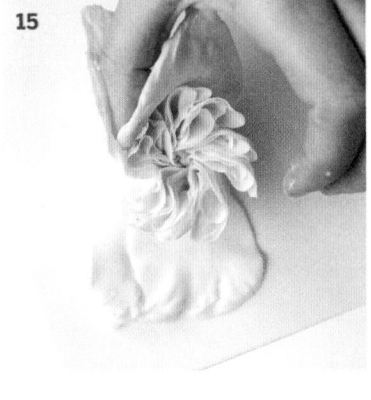

13 Set the larger petal set upside down on the craft foam pad so that the petals are curling toward the pad. Brush egg white on the center of the petal set and insert the flower. Brush egg white on one of the super petals, halfway up and along the entire right edge all the way up to the top.

14 Identify an opening in the inner petals. Slide the super petal into this open door, attaching that side firmly and allowing the left side of the petal to stay open.

15 Brush the smaller of the two remaining petals with egg white in the same way. Lift it up and place it as far into the door left open by petal 1 as possible. Attach firmly.

16 Repeat with the last super petal, placing it as far inside the door left open from petal 2. Pull each petal slightly as you "close" each door.

17 Repeat steps 10–16 with the 3 remaining large petal sets, working around the rose. Look for the open doors and place the petals as far

inside these doors as possible, then pull the petals across as you close the doors.

18 The layers and folds create their own shadows and highlights, so I recommend only very minimal dusting. Brush a complementary color petal dust lightly into the center and touch upon the outer petals to make sure everything is cohesive. Make sure to use a soft brush, as the petals are paper-thin and will chip if the bristles are too stiff.

19 In lieu of a gum paste calyx, add a bit of color by turning the flower over and brushing a bit of green at the base as well as down the stem a bit.

PEONY

TOOLS

- Gum paste in desired colors (small amount of white for centers, coral for petals)
- 24-gauge floral wire, cut into thirds
- Egg white in small dish
- Cornstarch in shaker
- Curved tweezers

- White floral tape
- GSA long pointed dull white tip stamens
- Zip-top bags
- CelBoard
- CelPin
- Round cutters (50mm, 65mm)

- CelPad 2
- Dresden tool
- JEM tool #12 (veining stick)
- Small paintbrushes
- Petal dusts in desired colors

1   Roll a tiny piece of white gum paste (the size of a peppercorn) into a smooth, oblong shape.

2   Moisten the end of an unhooked wire with a tiny bit of egg white. Insert the wire about two-thirds of the way into the gum paste. Dust your fingers with cornstarch and pinch the gum paste at the base so there is a good connection between the gum paste and the wire.

3   Use tweezers to pinch the tip of the gum paste to flatten it slightly and add some visual interest.

4   Repeat with 6 more pieces of gum paste and wires for a total of 7. Bring all these little guys together while they are still soft, being careful not to let them slide off the wires. Stretch a piece of floral tape to activate the nontoxic glue. Gather the wires and tape them together, starting as high as possible and working your way down at an angle. Pull the tape tightly as you go. Set aside and let dry for at least 1 hour.

5   Separate the stamens into four sections, as they can be a bit unruly to handle all at once. Align them so that the stamens sit slightly above the taped center. Wrap floral tape a few times around to secure the stamens.

6   Continue adding the stamens one section at a time, wrapping tightly as you go. Once the final section is in place, wrap with a fresh piece of floral tape, starting at the base of the stamen and working all the way down the wire so that everything is neat and contained. Set aside.

7   Massage a small piece of coral gum paste and press it into the center of the CelBoard with cornstarch-dusted fingers. Take your time, patting the piece down to ensure that it is firmly pressed into the groove of the board. Use the CelPin to roll the gum paste, beginning in the center and using short motions. Don't worry about rolling all the way out to the edges of the paste. The piece needs only to be long enough and wide enough to cut a single petal. (I find it too time-consuming to make the paste even enough from top to bottom to make more than one cut.)

8   Continue rolling until you can just barely make out the center line from the groove in the board beneath. The paste should feel even and smooth. After a bit of practice, you'll get a sense of the right thickness. Peel the paste out of the board and set it vein-side up on your work surface. Use a 50mm cutter to cut out a round and place it in a zip-top bag. Quickly massage the remaining scrap piece, introduce more gum paste as needed, and repeat to make a total of 10 small rounds. Repeat steps 7 and 8, using the 65mm cutter to cut 5 large rounds. Place them in a zip-top bag as you work. If you'd like, cut a few extra small and large rounds— it's always a good idea to make extra petals in case of breakage or a shape that doesn't quite fit in.

9   Dip the end of a wire into a bit of egg white and insert the wire into the thickest part of the vein in one petal until it is about two-thirds of the way into the round. As you are inserting the wire, hold your thumb at the top and place another finger underneath so that you can feel if the wire is getting too close to the top or bottom. Adjust the alignment so the wire doesn't poke through. Once the wire is in place, give a little pinch at the base of the petal to be sure it's secure.

10   Place the petal on the CelPad, vein-side down. Brace the petal with your nondominant hand and use the CelPin to thin and stretch it. As always, apply the most pressure to the edge of the petal.

11   Point the wire away from you. Align the point of the veining stick toward the bottom of the petal. Apply pressure and roll slightly following the curve of the petal to create veins that radiate from the midpoint where the wire meets the petal. Avoid rolling directly over the center wire.

12   Place the flatter side of the Dresden tool just before the edge of the petal. Brace the petal with your nondominant hand and apply a bit of pressure as you make your way around the petal edge. The edge should curl gently inward.

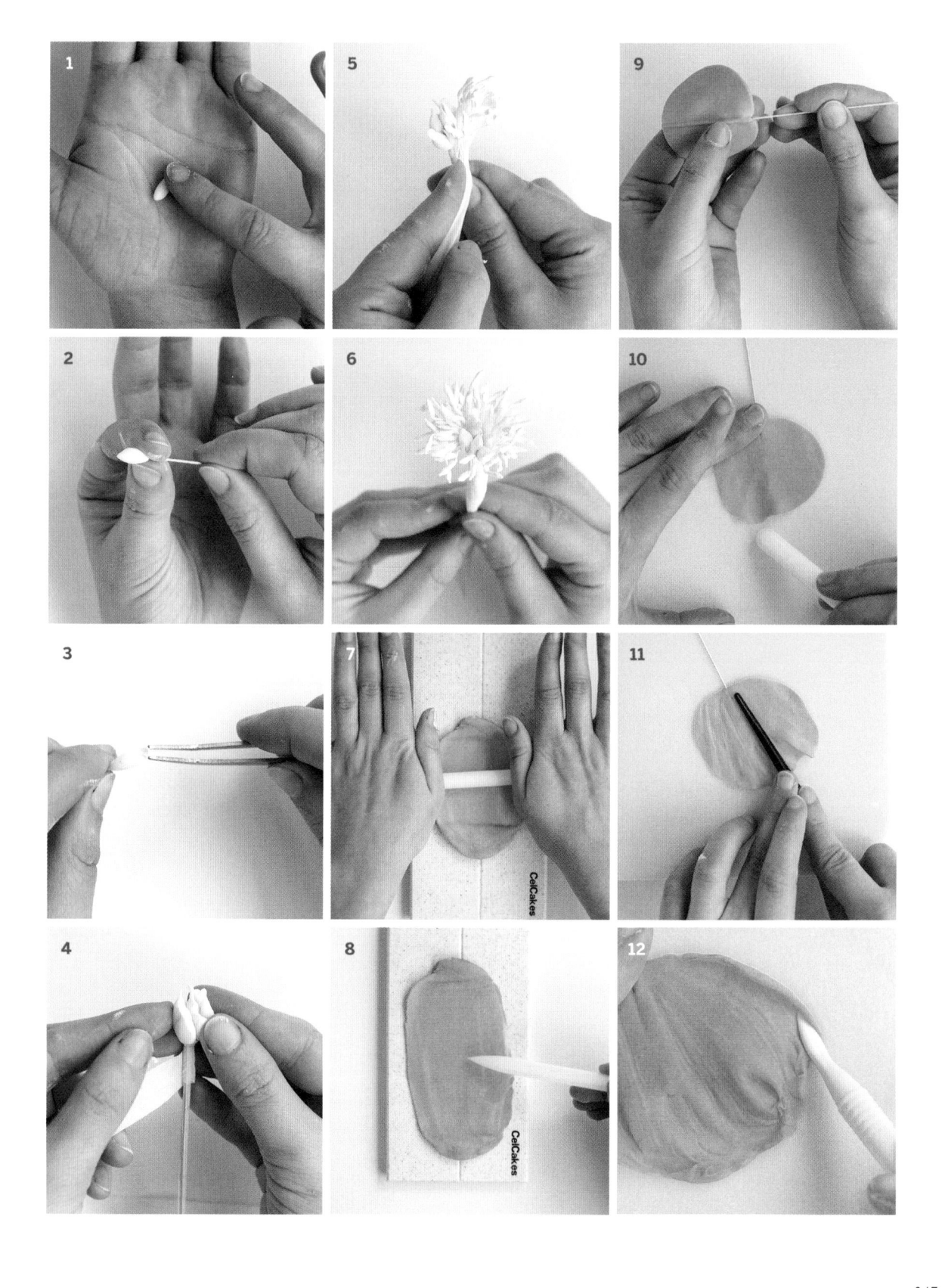

13 Gently cup the petal and check the connection at the base to make sure the petal and wire are still secure. Lay the petal on slightly scrunched aluminum foil or parchment paper for a petal that's slightly cupped, or simply let it dry flat on your workstation for a petal that is completely open. It's nice to have a variety of shapes so you have some options when it comes time to assemble. Repeat to shape the rest of the petals. Let dry for a few hours or overnight.

14 Have all your components dry and ready for assembly. I prefer to keep my center uncolored at this stage, as I like to see the fully assembled flower before adding color. If you have a very clear plan for your finished colors, you can certainly color the petals and the center before assembly.

15 Begin with the small inner petals. Angle the petal back from the wire so it's easier to align with the peony center's wire. Wrap floral tape tightly around the wire a couple of times before adding more petals. I usually introduce no more than 3 petals at a time before taping a bit.

16 Continue adding the remaining smaller petals, then add the larger petals for the outer layers. Don't worry about the placement of the petals as you tape.

17 Once all the petals are secure, continue wrapping the tape down the wire at a slight angle. You can now move the petals around and open and close them as you like.

18 Brush the center of the peony with a bit of green petal dust. Brush the stamens with golden yellow. It's okay if a bit of the yellow dust gets on the base of the petals.

19 Carefully touch a bit of hot pink dust on the pinched edges of the peony center.

20 Brush a bit of pink and/or yellow petal dust on a few areas on the petals to emphasize the coral color. Brush green and brown dust at the base of the flower and down the stem.

CATTLEYA ORCHID

TOOLS

- Gum paste in desired colors (white for column, raspberry pink for lip, lime green for sepals and petals)
- 22-gauge white floral wire, cut into thirds
- Cornstarch in shaker
- Dresden tool
- Pasta roller

- Crystal Flowers small Cattleya orchid cutter set of 3
- CelPad 2
- JEM tool #12 (veining stick)
- Curved tweezers
- Small paintbrushes
- Egg white in small dish

- CelBoard
- Medium CelPin
- 28-gauge white floral wire, cut into quarters
- White floral tape
- Petal dusts in desired colors
- Vodka in dropper bottle

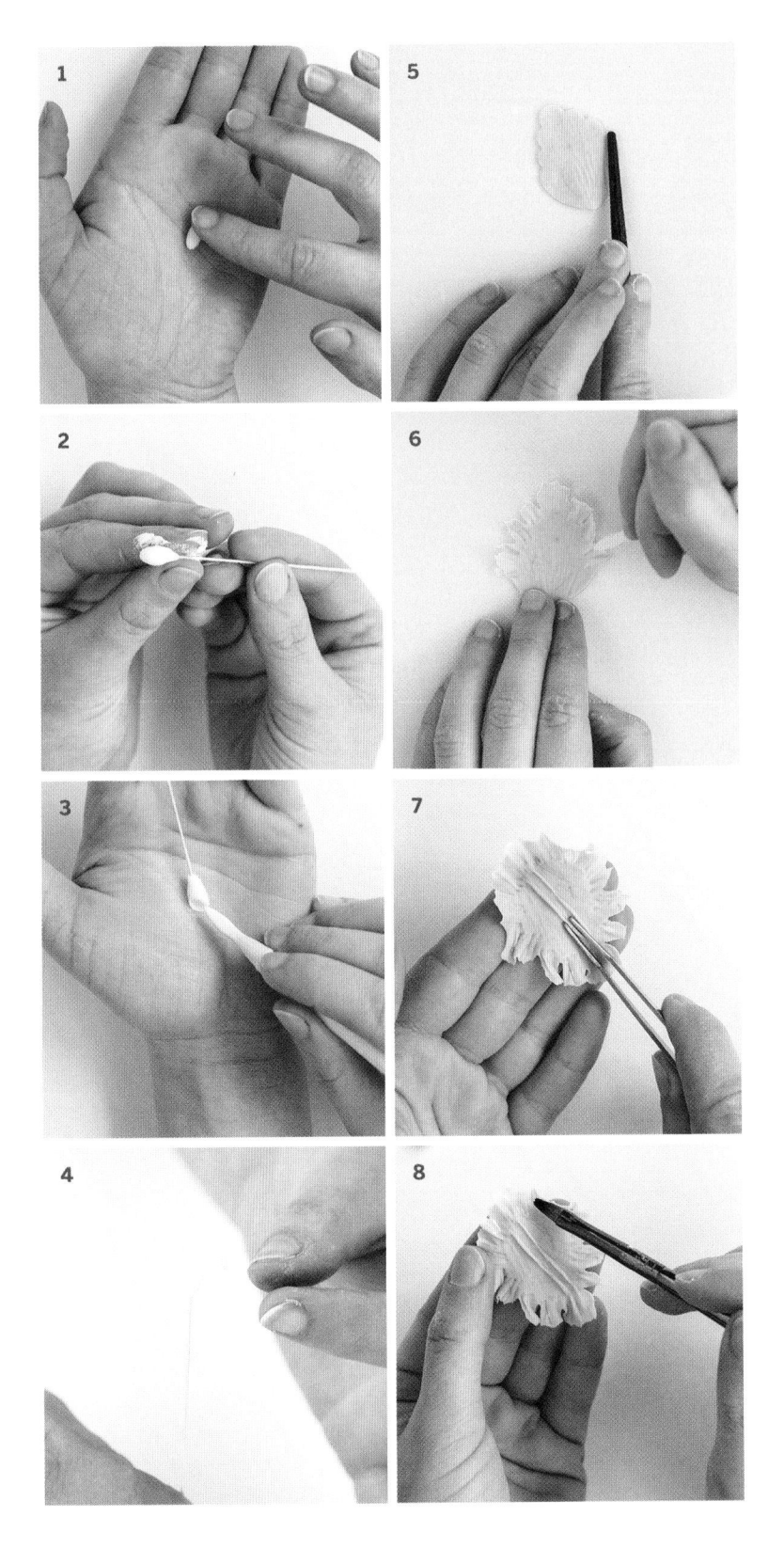

1 To make the column, roll a tiny piece of white gum paste (about the size of a peppercorn) into a smooth, oblong shape.

2 Moisten the end of a piece of 22-gauge wire with a tiny bit of egg white, wipe off any excess, and insert the wire about two-thirds of the way into the gum paste. Use cornstarch-dusted fingers to pinch at the base so there is a good connection between the gum paste and the wire.

3 Use the flatter end of a Dresden tool to hollow out the top one-third of the gum paste. This will push the paste a bit toward the top edge, so be sure to go back and thin it a bit.

4 Use two fingers to pinch a little beak so that the top points down slightly and tapers. Insert the stem into a Styrofoam block and let dry for at least 4 hours or preferably overnight.

5 Use a pasta roller to roll the pink gum paste to a thinness of level 5. Make a single cut with the orchid set's scalloped cutter. We'll call this piece the "lip." Place it on a CelPad and use the veining stick to create veins, starting at one side with the stick pointing toward the outer edge and rotating the stick as you press and roll so that the veins radiate outward from the base.

6 Bracing the lip with your opposite hand, use the Dresden tool to form tightly spaced frills on the edge of the lip all the way around.

7 Hold the lip and use tweezers to pinch two distinct ridges down the center.

8 Brush a tiny bit of egg white on either side of the base of the lip.

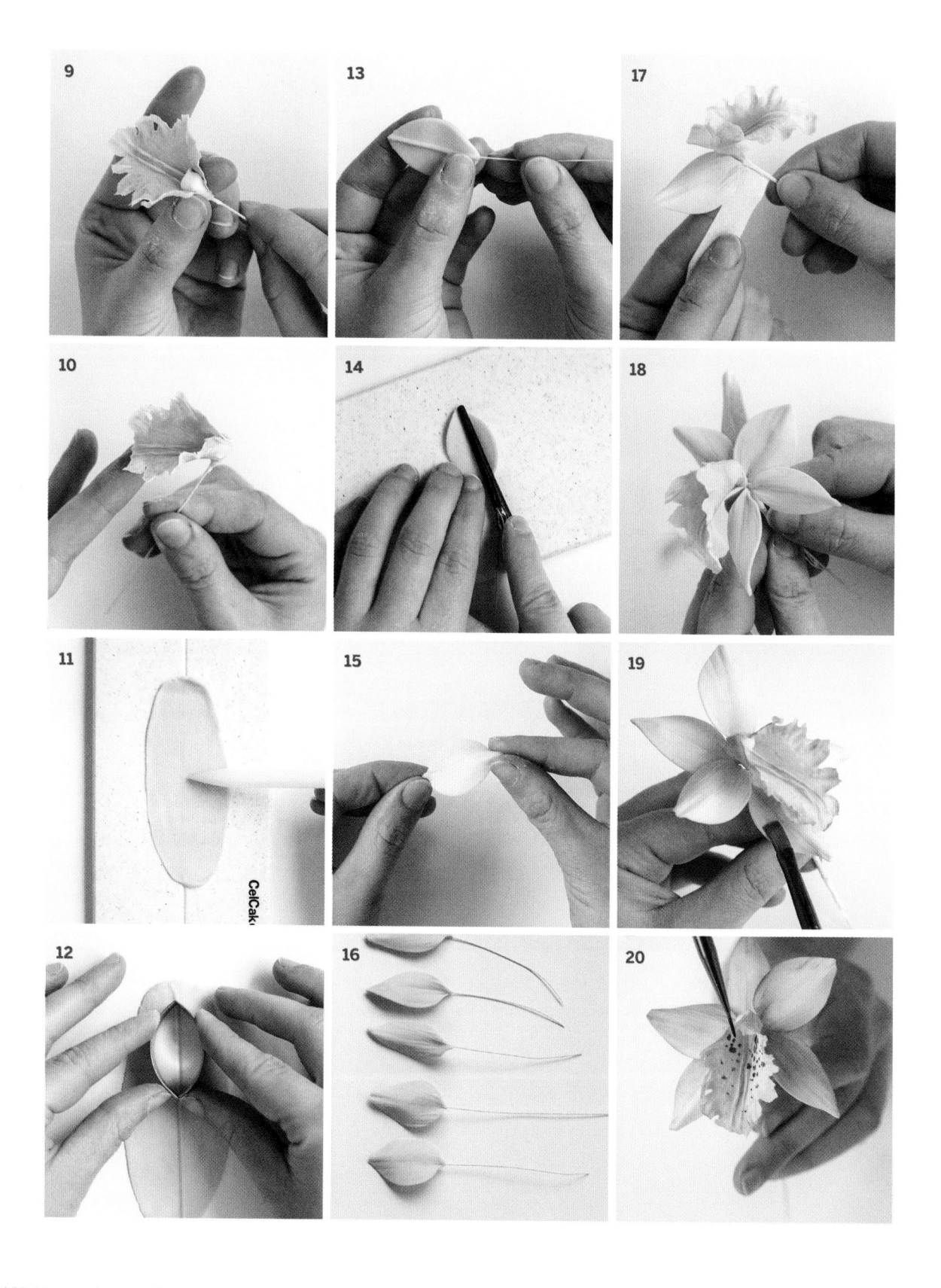

9 Place the dry orchid column so the beak is pointing down toward the tweezed ridges. Bring the edges up and around the little stem and back of the beak and attach firmly, pressing down any seams that may form.

10 Using your finger, gently encourage the lowest, tapered section of the frilled lip to curve slightly downward. Insert the wire in the Styrofoam and let dry for at least 2 hours.

11 Massage a small piece of green gum paste and, with cornstarch-dusted fingers, press it into the center of the CelBoard. Press down firmly to ensure that it stays in the groove of the board. Roll out the gum paste with the CelPin. Use short rolling motions to get started, then continue rolling until the gum paste is even and smooth and you can just make out the center line from the groove in the board beneath.

12 Turn out the gum paste onto your work surface so the vein is facing up. Use the wider petal cutter from the set to cut out 2 petals. Keep them in a zip-top bag while you work with one at a time. Quickly massage the scrap piece of gum paste and either re-roll it or place it in a zip-top bag.

13 Dip one end of a 28-gauge wire in egg white, wipe off any excess, and insert the wire into the thickest part of the vein in one petal so it comes about two-thirds of the way up the petal. If you notice the wire coming through, pull back slightly and redirect. Pinch gently at the base to ensure a good connection between the gum paste and the wire.

14 Place the petal on the back of the CelBoard so you have a smooth, hard surface and use the veining stick to create veins radiating from the base of the petal. (Doing this on a hard surface results in more distinct veining.)

15 Pinch gently at the top to give the petal movement and at the base to ensure the wire is secure. Insert the stem into the Styrofoam and let dry for at least 2 hours. Repeat steps 13–15 with the second cut-out petal.Repeat steps 11–15, using the narrower cutter from the set, to make 3 sepals. If you'd like, cut a few extra petals and sepals—it's always a good idea to make a couple extra in case of breakage!

16 When you are ready to assemble the orchid, have all the components dry and ready for taping. If you are more comfortable painting the individual pieces before assembly, this would be the time to do it.

17 Align the wires of the two petals with the center wire. Stretch a piece of floral tape to activate the nontoxic glue and wrap the tape tightly around the wires a couple of times.

18 Add the sepals and continue taping down the wire. Once secure, arrange the pieces so the two petals are pointing out at an angle, one sepal is straight up at the top, and the other two are pointing down at slight angles from the frilled lip.

19 Edge the frilled lip with lime-green petal dust. Touch the same color to the tweezed ridges. Brush the petals and sepals with a bit of lime-green dust and edge with hot pink, particularly at the points.

20 Add a few drops of vodka to a mix of fuchsia and hot pink petal dusts to make a liquid paint. Use a fine-tip brush to make dots of various sizes inside the lip and randomly, though less concentrated, on the sepals and petals. Brush green and brown dust at the base of the flower as well as down the stem.

AFTER KILLING MANY LIVE ORCHIDS, I decided to make some out of sugar instead. This arrangement was a gift for my husband's birthday and, even though he is constantly surrounded by my work, it took him a minute or two to realize they were handmade. Granted, the lighting was low and we were drinking champagne.

Like the orchids on page 250, the graceful Phalaenopsis is constructed with a sculpted center and individually wired petals that are then taped together. Here a fondant-covered Styrofoam cube acts as the vessel. I cut leaves free-form and veined them using the side of a Dresden tool. The branches are sturdy 18-gauge wires taped together, inserted into the Styrofoam as far as they can go for support.

ANEMONE

TOOLS

- 20-gauge white floral wire, cut into thirds
- White floral tape
- Gum paste in desired colors (black for the center, blush lavender for petals)
- Egg white in small dish
- Cornstarch in shaker
- Craft knife, such as X-ACTO
- Styrofoam block
- Edible marker, such as AmeriColor Food Writer (black)
- Round piping tip or 25mm round cutter
- Wafer paper
- Small paintbrushes
- Spring-action scissors
- Pasta roller
- JEM 50mm Easy Rose Cutter
- Zip-top bags
- CelPad 2
- Medium CelPin
- JEM tool #12 (veining stick)
- Craft foam square
- Petal dusts in desired colors

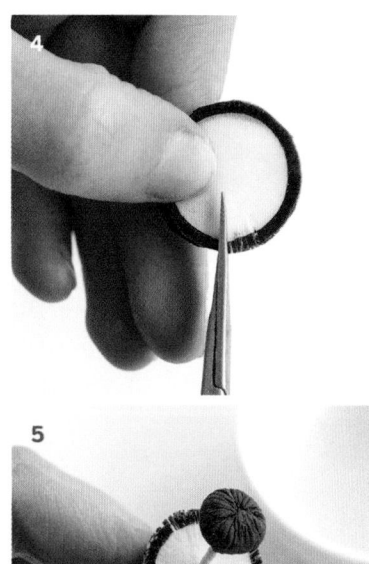

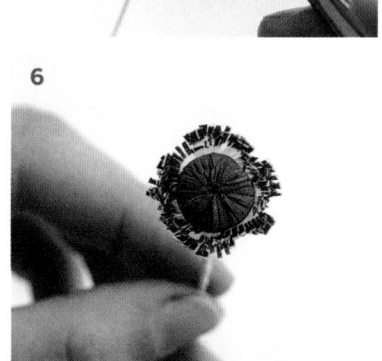

the gum paste and the wire. Don't be concerned if the entire taped hook is not covered by the gum paste. While the gum paste is still soft, use a craft knife to make very shallow slices radiating outward from the center.

2 Continue the shallow slicing all the way around. Insert the stem into a block of Styrofoam and let dry overnight.

3 Using black edible marker, trace the outside of the wide end of a piping tip (or a 25mm round cutter) on wafer paper. You will need 2 circles per anemone. Turn the paper over and trace the circles you just made on the other side.

4 Carefully cut out each circle. Place a tiny (really tiny) dot of egg white in the center of one circle and place the second circle on top. Any kind of moisture will cause the wafer paper to break down, so it's crucial that you use the smallest amount of egg white possible to connect the pieces just in the center. Use scissors to snip into the stacked circles, cutting about one-quarter of the way toward the center. Continue snipping all the way around.

5 Insert the flower center through the center of the wafer paper and slide the snipped circles halfway up the wire. Pause to brush a very small amount of egg white in the center of the wafer paper.

6 Slide the circles all the way up the wire and gently press to attach them to the base of the gum paste center. Insert the stem into the Styrofoam and let dry as you work on the petals.

1 Prep the wire by bending a small closed loop as shown on page 231. Wrap the wire with floral tape, taping a few times around the loop before continuing down the wire at a slight angle. Roll a smooth ball of black gum paste the size of a small grape (about 1.5 grams). Dip just the tip

of the prepared wire in a little egg white, wipe off any excess, and insert the wire into the ball until you can feel the wire close to the top of the gum paste. Flip the wire and pinch the gum paste at the base with cornstarch-dusted fingers to ensure a good connection between

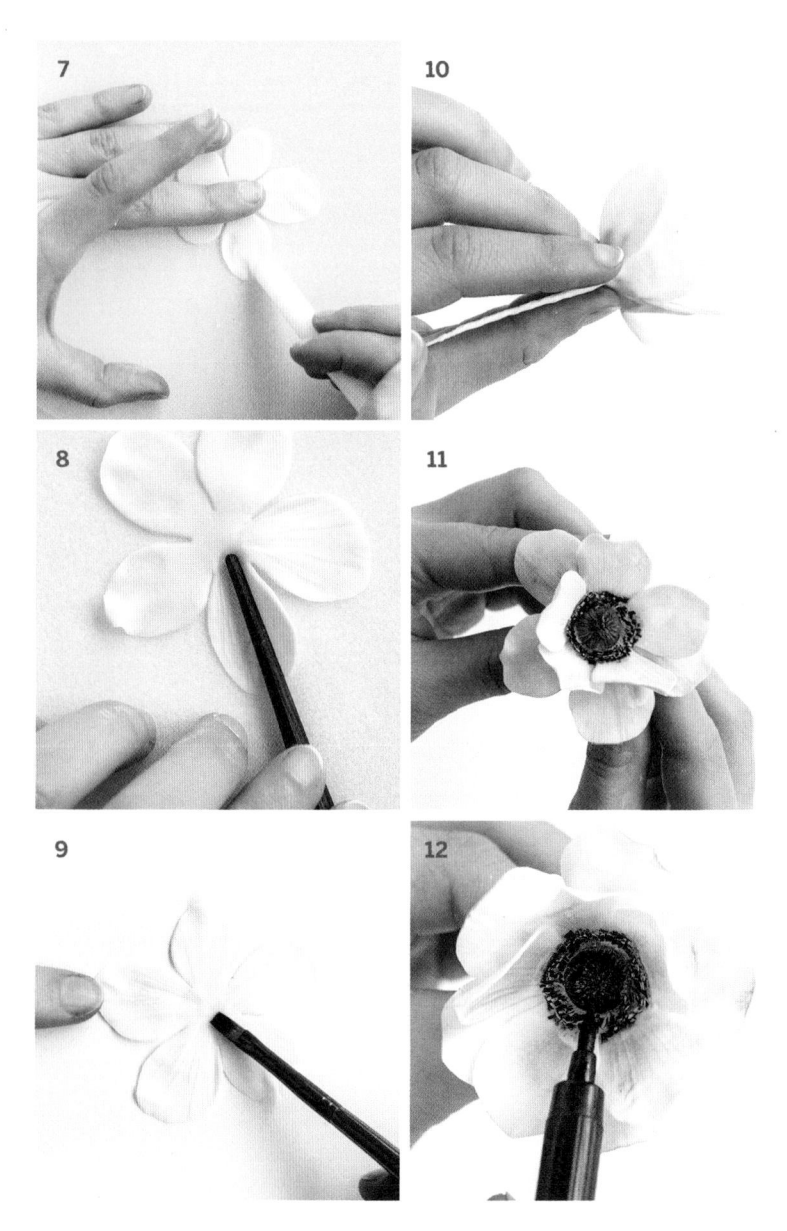

9 Transfer the petal set to a craft foam square and brush egg white in the center, making sure to coat all the way out to where the base of the petals joins the center of the set.

10 Insert the flower center through the center of the petal set on the foam square. Flip upside down and remove the foam square. Gently press at the base to be sure the petal set is well attached to the center. Bend the wire so the petals stay upside down. Insert the stem into the Styrofoam and let dry for at least 2 hours before adding the second set. This inner set of petals will cup slightly around the center, so there will be a distinct difference in appearance between the first set of petals and the second.

11 Repeat steps 7–9 with the second set of petals. Insert the single-layer flower through the center of the petals on the foam square, then remove the foam. Press gently at the base to secure the petals. Insert the stem into the Styrofoam and let dry either upside down or sideways, depending on how open or closed you wish the final flower to be. Let dry for at least 2 hours or preferably overnight before applying color. Use a soft brush to apply lavender petal dust close to the center and fanning out slightly.

12 Use the edible marker to intensify the color of the black center. Brush a bit of green and brown petal dust underneath the flower and down the stem.

7 Use a pasta roller to roll the lavender gum paste to a thinness of level 6. Cut out two sets of petals with the rose cutter. Place one set in a zip-top bag and the other set on the CelPad. Bracing the petal set with your nondominant hand, thin each petal using the CelPin by brushing outward over the edge of the petal.

8 Vein each petal using a veining stick; the veins should start at the base and radiate outward. Starting at one side of the petal, apply pressure and roll the veining stick to create veins, then rotate the tool to move around the petal.

HYDRANGEA

TOOLS

- 26-gauge green floral wire, cut into quarters
- Gum paste in desired color (blue-purple)
- CelPad (with holes)
- Cornstarch in shaker
- Medium CelPin
- GSA hydrangea petal cutter
- Zip-top bags
- JEM tool #12 (veining stick)
- Egg white in small dish
- Styrofoam block
- Small paintbrushes
- Petal dusts in desired colors

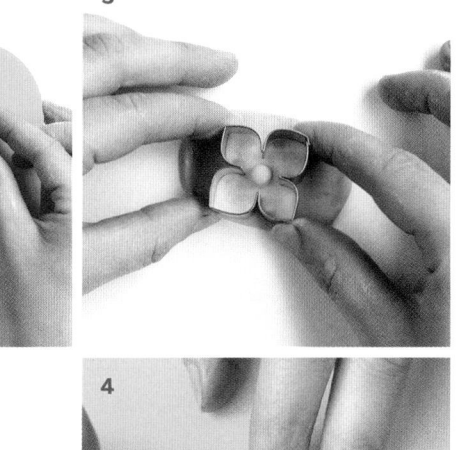

1

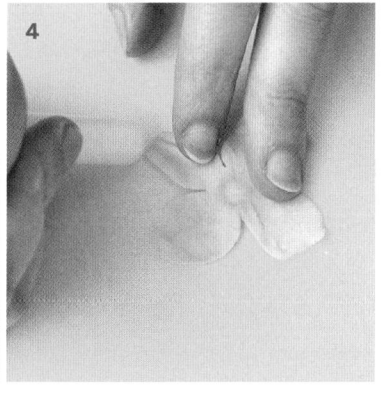

3

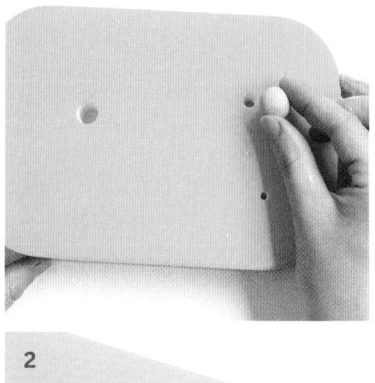

2

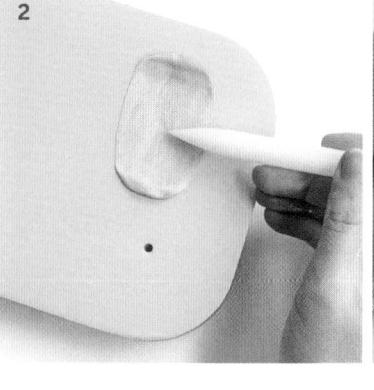

4

1   Prep the wire by bending a tiny hook at one end. Roll a small amount of the colored gum paste (about the size of a small grape) into a smooth ball. Identify the medium-size hole on the orange side of the CelPad.

2   Dust your fingers with cornstarch, press the ball firmly over the medium hole, and squish it down until flattened a bit. Roll out the paste using the CelPin. Use short rolling movements at first to get it started, and then work out toward the edges. This method helps to keep the paste from lifting out of the hole and compromising the "stem." Continue rolling until you can just start to see the shape of the hole underneath. Don't worry about the paste building up on the edges; you only need enough flat surface to make a single cut with the hydrangea cutter.

3   Peel the gum paste out and place it on your work surface, stem-side up. Center the cutter over the stem and cut out a petal set. Immediately pick up the little scraps, massage them together, and place them in a zip-top bag.

4   Turn the CelPad over to the softer (yellow) side. Place the stem in the large hole. This acts as a support as you thin the petals. Brace the petal set with your nondominant hand and use the CelPin to thin the petals, brushing from the center outward and over the edge of the petals, applying the most pressure as you exit the petal. If your petals are cupping, that means you are stopping prematurely.

5 Hold the veining stick pointing toward the center of the petal. Starting at one side of each petal, press down and roll to the center to create veins, then rotate the tool to move around the petal. Repeat with all the petals.

6 Remove the petal set from the CelPad. Dip the nonhooked end of the wire into egg white, wipe off any excess, and insert it into the center of the flower from the top.

7 Pull the wire down so that it goes through the center of the stem and continue until there is just a tiny bit of the green hook still visible.

8 Place your fingers underneath all four petals and give one good pinch. If you find the center is not clearly defined, or there is a buildup of gum paste, that's a good indication that you didn't roll the gum paste thin enough on the orange side of the CelPad. Try again with another flower. This takes practice! Insert the stem into a block of Styrofoam and let dry overnight. For a closed flower, bend the wire so the flower hangs down over the edge of the Styrofoam.

For half open, bend the wire so the flower is facing out, sideways. For fully open, take advantage of gravity by having all petals spread out and upside down on the work surface with the stem inserted into the side of the Styrofoam for a little support.

9 Use a soft brush to apply a mix of blue and purple petal dusts to the fully dry petals.

10 Layer with green petal dust here and there. See page 281 to learn how to make "packets" and bring several together for a full cluster of hydrangea.

A SPECIAL DAY denoted by decidedly festive lapels—fait accompli with these sweet boutonnieres. Almost any diminutive sugar flower, bud, or sprig of greenery can be used; this assortment includes rose, orchid, tiny peony buds, hydrangea, ranunculus, and anemone. This can be a good way to make use of any spare or mismatched sprigs you may have in your sugar-flower "garden." Wrap the combined stems in floral tape, and then finish with a knotted ribbon.

RANUNCULUS

TOOLS

- 18-gauge white floral wire, cut into thirds
- White floral tape
- Pasta roller
- Gum paste in desired colors (black for center, white for petals)
- JEM 50mm Easy Rose Cutter
- Zip-top bags
- CelBoard
- JEM tool #12 (veining stick)
- Cornstarch in shaker
- Craft foam square with hole cut in center
- Small paintbrushes
- Egg white in small dish
- Styrofoam block
- JEM 60mm Easy Rose Cutter
- Petal dusts in desired colors

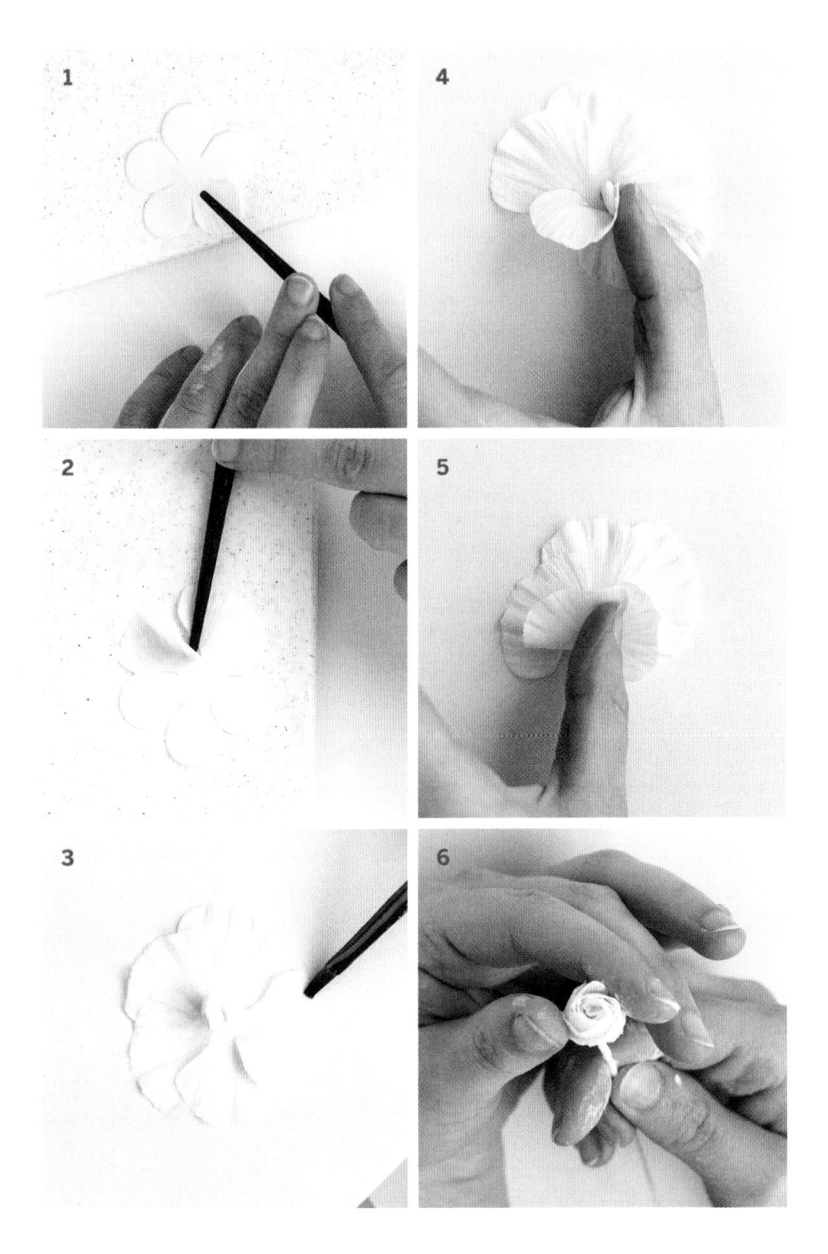

1 Prepare the wire by bending a closed loop at one end as shown on page 231. Wrap with floral tape, taping about 8 times around the loop before continuing down the wire at a slight angle. The end result, which looks a bit like a Q-tip, is a tiny center on which you will build the flower. Use a pasta roller to roll white gum paste to a thinness of level 6. Using a 50mm rose cutter, cut out 4 petal sets and place them in a zip-top bag. Turn the CelBoard over so that the plain side is facing up. Place a petal set close to the edge. Use the veining stick to vein the petals: Point the veining stick toward the center at an angle with the back end of the stick off the board.

This placement will give you extra leverage to apply a lot of pressure and get a deep impression. Starting at one side of each petal, press down and roll to the center to create veins, then rotate the tool to move around the petal.

2 The veined petal should be significantly larger and wider and translucent. Lift each previous petal and fold it slightly out of the way so that you can vein the petal next door without disturbing the first.

3 Continue veining all the petals and then transfer the petal set to a craft foam square with a hole in the center. Brush egg white in the center of the petal set. Insert the wire stem downward through the center of the petal set through the hole in the center of the board. Brush egg white at the base of one petal (it doesn't matter which one you start with) and just a bit higher on the right edge.

4 Lift up the petal and attach the right edge to the taped center, wrapping it around the center. Keep the left side open, like a door.

5 Working clockwise, apply egg white to the next petal, at the base and up the right edge. Lift up the petal, slide the right edge as far into the open "door" of the previous petal as possible, and wrap it around the taped center, again leaving the left edge open like a door.

6 Continue lifting up and attaching all the petals until you have a complete spiral. Remove the flower from the foam square. Without squeezing, gently adjust the petals to close all of the doors.

7 With your fingers dusted with plenty of cornstarch, pinch gently at the base so there is a secure connection to the wire. Because the taped center is so small, it's very important that you do a good job of securing this first layer. Insert the stem into a block of Styrofoam and let dry overnight.

8 Prepare three more small petal sets as described in steps 1–3. Lift up and attach each petal as described in steps 4–5; look for an "open door" from the dry first layer to start and then continue tucking each subsequent petal into the open door of the previous petal as closely as possible. Gently adjust the petals to close all the doors, secure at the base, and let dry for about 1 hour.

9 Repeat step 8, this time using the 60mm rose cutter to cut out four more petal sets. Continue arranging the petals in the same way. The very last set can be left slightly more open. Don't be afraid of asymmetry! To me, a couple of extra petals off to one side are more beautiful than something perfectly round and tidy.

10 With a small, soft brush, tap a very small amount of green petal dust into the very center of the flower. If you accidentally add too much, have cream or white dust on hand to layer over it.

11 Lightly touch a few of the petal edges with green, brown, and cream petal dusts.

12 Brush green and brown petal dusts underneath the flower and down the stem.

CLOVER

TOOLS

- 26-gauge green floral wire, cut into thirds
- Pasta roller
- Gum paste in desired colors (fuchsia for petals, green for calyx)

- FMM daisy cutter set
- Zip-top bags
- CelPad 2
- Dresden tool
- Small paintbrush

- Egg white in a small dish
- Cornstarch in shaker
- Styrofoam
- Spring-action scissors

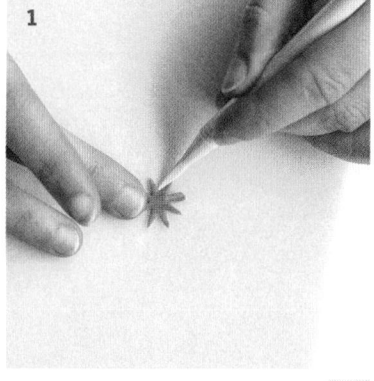

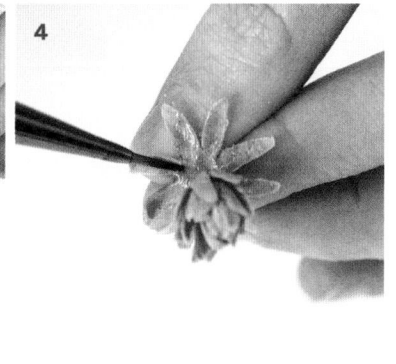

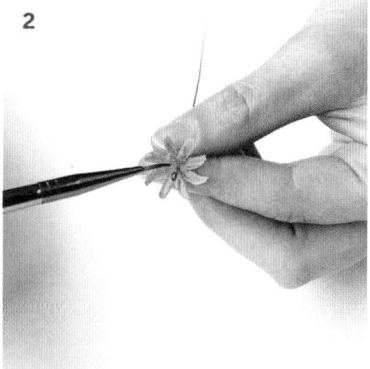

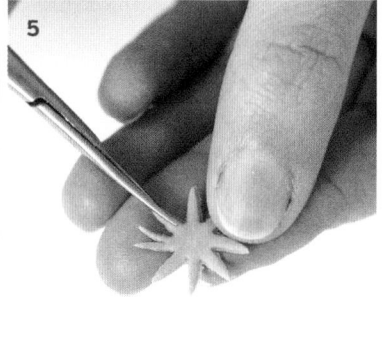

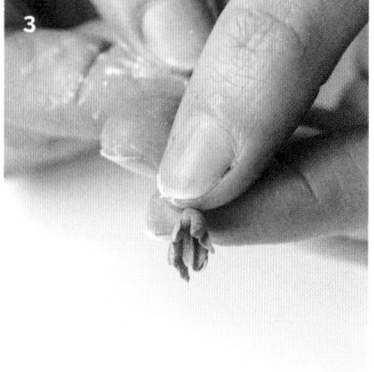

2   Remove the petal set from the CelPad and insert the non-looped end of the wire through the center. Slide the petals up the wire until you reach the base of the loop and dab a tiny amount of egg white just on the center of the petal set.

3   Pinch the petals so they close gently around the loop (which is acting as your center). Dust your fingers with cornstarch and pinch at the base to secure. Insert the stem into a Styrofoam block and let dry for at least 1 hour before adding more layers.

4   Make five more layers of petals as described in steps 1–3, with a dab of egg white in between each set. These can be placed consecutively, without drying time in between. You'll find that as the clover gets bigger, the petal sets start to sit lower on the flower. This is what you want! Instead of getting wider and wider, it starts to taper, naturally.

5   For the calyx, use a pasta roller to roll green gum paste to a thinness of level 6. Cut a single piece using the small daisy cutter. Use scissors to snip straight down the center of each little petal.

6   Apply a dab of egg white to the center of the calyx and slide it up underneath the clover. Insert the stem into the Styrofoam and let dry for about 1 hour before coloring, if desired.

1   Prepare a wire by bending a tiny closed loop at one end. Use a pasta roller to roll fuchsia gum paste to a thinness of level 6. Using the small daisy cutter, cut out 6 petal sets and store them in zip-top bags. Work with one petal set at a time. Place the first set on the CelPad. Brace the petal set with your nondominant hand and use the narrowest side of the Dresden tool to gently thin each petal by brushing outward over the petal edge.

GREENERY

TOOLS

ALL GREENERY

+ Gum paste in desired colors (such as medium green, light green, barely green)
+ Cornstarch in shaker
+ CelBoard
+ Medium CelPin
+ Zip-top bags
+ Egg white in small dish
+ Styrofoam block
+ Petal dust in desired colors
+ Small paintbrushes
+ Vodka in dropper bottle (optional)

ROSE LEAF

+ Leaf cutter
+ 26-gauge green floral wire, cut into thirds
+ CK rose leaf silicone veiner mold

LITTLE GREEN LEAF

+ Crystal Flowers sepal cutter, Sunflower Sugar Art rose leaf cutter, or other small leaf or petal cutter
+ 26-gauge green floral wire, cut into quarters
+ Sunflower Sugar Art rose leaf cutter set (or any small leaf or petal cutter)

LAMB'S EAR

+ 26-gauge green floral wire, cut into thirds
+ Craft knife, such as X-ACTO
+ Large very soft paintbrush

BABY EUCALYPTUS

+ Round piping tips (15mm and 20mm), or 15mm and 20mm round cutters
+ CK rose leaf silicone veiner mold
+ 20-gauge white floral wire, uncut
+ Small Cattleya orchid cutter set

ROSE LEAF

1 Massage a small piece of medium-green gum paste and with cornstarch-dusted fingers press it into the center of the CelBoard. Press down firmly to ensure that it stays in the groove of the board. Roll out the gum paste using the CelPin: Use short rolling motions to get started, then continue rolling until the gum paste is even and smooth and you can just make out the center line from the groove in the board underneath.

2 Turn out the gum paste onto your work surface so the vein is facing up. Use the rose leaf cutter to cut out leaves, placing them in a zip-top bag as you go. Be sure to quickly massage the scrap piece of gum paste and either reroll it or place it in a zip-top bag.

3 Dip one end of a 26-gauge wire in egg white and then insert the wire into the thickest part of the vein at the bottom of the leaf, pushing it about two-thirds of the way up the leaf. If you feel the wire coming through the gum paste, pull back slightly and redirect. Pinch gently at the base to ensure a good connection between the gum paste and the wire.

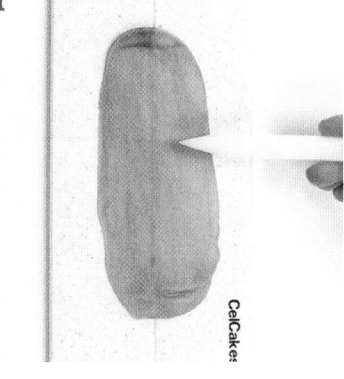

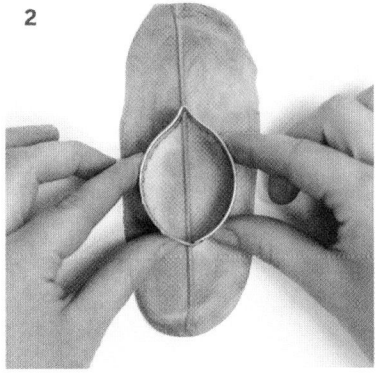

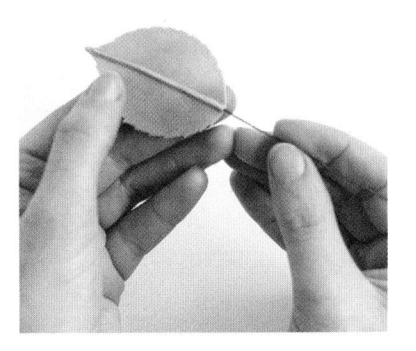

4 Place the leaf vein-side down into the base of the silicone rose leaf mold and cover with the top piece. (If your mold is brand-new, or if you find the leaf is difficult to remove, you may need to "season" it with just a tiny bit of shortening.) Press down firmly.

5 Remove the top piece and carefully peel the leaf out of the mold. If you have a tiny hole in your leaf, good for you! That kind of imperfection makes it more interesting. If you can see the wire through the leaf, don't panic. The petal dust will hide it.

6 Pinch the leaf at the base to secure the wire. Give the leaf a little pinch or twist to give it some personality. Insert the stem into a Styrofoam block and let dry for a few hours or preferably overnight before coloring or assembling.

7 Apply a moss green dust to parts of the leaf.

8 Use chocolate brown dust to tap color into the base of the leaf and draw slightly up the center seam. Highlight with a little white petal dust. It can be lovely to add in a little bit of color here along with the white. For example, if these leaves will accompany yellow roses, brush a tiny bit of yellow dust over the white area.

LITTLE GREEN LEAF

1   Roll out, cut, and wire the leaf as described in steps 1–3 (see page 273) for a rose leaf, using a sepal cutter or small leaf cutter and a shorter 26-gauge wire (cut into quarters). Once the wire is inserted, hold the leaf so the side where the wire was inserted is facing away from you. Pinch at the base as usual, but also pinch the leaf inward, creating a defined center seam. Pinch a bit at the top and pull back very slightly to add some movement. Insert the stem into a Styrofoam block and let dry for at least a few hours or preferably overnight.

2   Brush lime green petal dust on one side.

3   Brush bright yellow petal dust on the other.

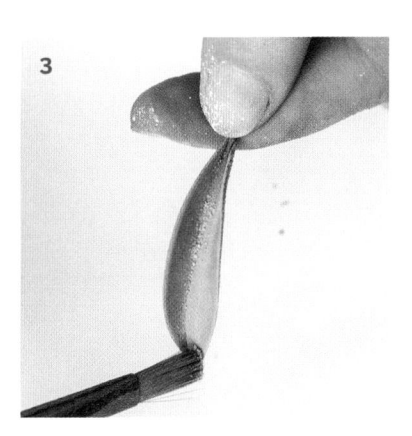

LAMB'S EAR

1   Give the palest green gum paste a mini massage and press it into a paddle shape on the CelBoard. This leaf is made without a cutter, so try to keep the shape intact. Roll it very gently with a CelPin. Unlike other leaves, this one needs to stay pretty thick.

2   Peel the leaf off the board. Dip one end of a 26-gauge wire (cut in thirds) in egg white, and then insert the wire into the narrow end of the leaf. Pinch at the base to ensure a secure connection and use your fingers to taper the leaf slightly at the top. Set the leaf on your work surface with the wire pointing away from you. Holding the base of the leaf gently, use a craft knife to mimic the veins of a leaf: Make a shallow slice (just breaking the surface) down the center and slashes at angles.

3   The finished leaf has the look of being plush and soft. Check the connection at the base to make sure it is secure. Insert the stem into a Styrofoam block and let dry overnight.

4   Use a large, very soft brush to cover the leaf in white petal dust. Be sure to hold the leaf over your work surface, in the same place, so that you can reuse the dust that falls.

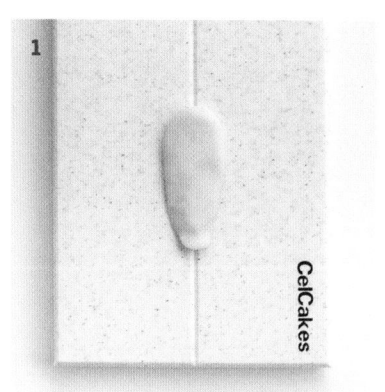

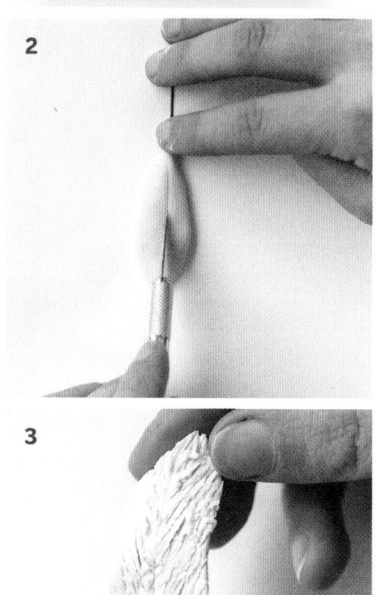

BABY EUCALYPTUS

1   Use a pasta roller to roll light green gum paste to a thinness of level 6. Use the narrow end of 15mm and 20mm plain piping tips or round cutters to cut out about 15 circles (cut a roughly equal number of smaller and larger rounds). Place them in a zip-top bag.

2   Work with one round at a time. Place a round on the base of the rose leaf mold. Press gently to vein lightly.

3   Paint a tiny amount of egg white on the base of the round.

4   Pinch the moistened area around one end of a 20-gauge white floral wire (uncut), close to the top. Dust your fingertips with cornstarch if the paste is sticky. It's okay to form a tiny "tail" of gum paste along the wire. Pull back very gently so that the leaf is sitting just shy of perpendicular to the wire. This is a delicate process, and it takes a little practice to find a rhythm.

5   Repeat steps 2–4 using the smaller rounds, placing one leaf opposite the other (or slightly below), followed by a gap of exposed wire. Use the bigger rounds as you move farther down the wire. Insert the stem into the Styrofoam and let dry for a few hours.

6   Use a soft brush (remember, these are very fragile!) to apply green petal dust in a few areas to add shading. Add white petal dust for highlights.

7–8   Carefully brush green petal dust on the exposed wire. Or, for more precise and saturated color, add a few drops of vodka to the petal dust to make a paint and apply it to the wire with a fine brush.

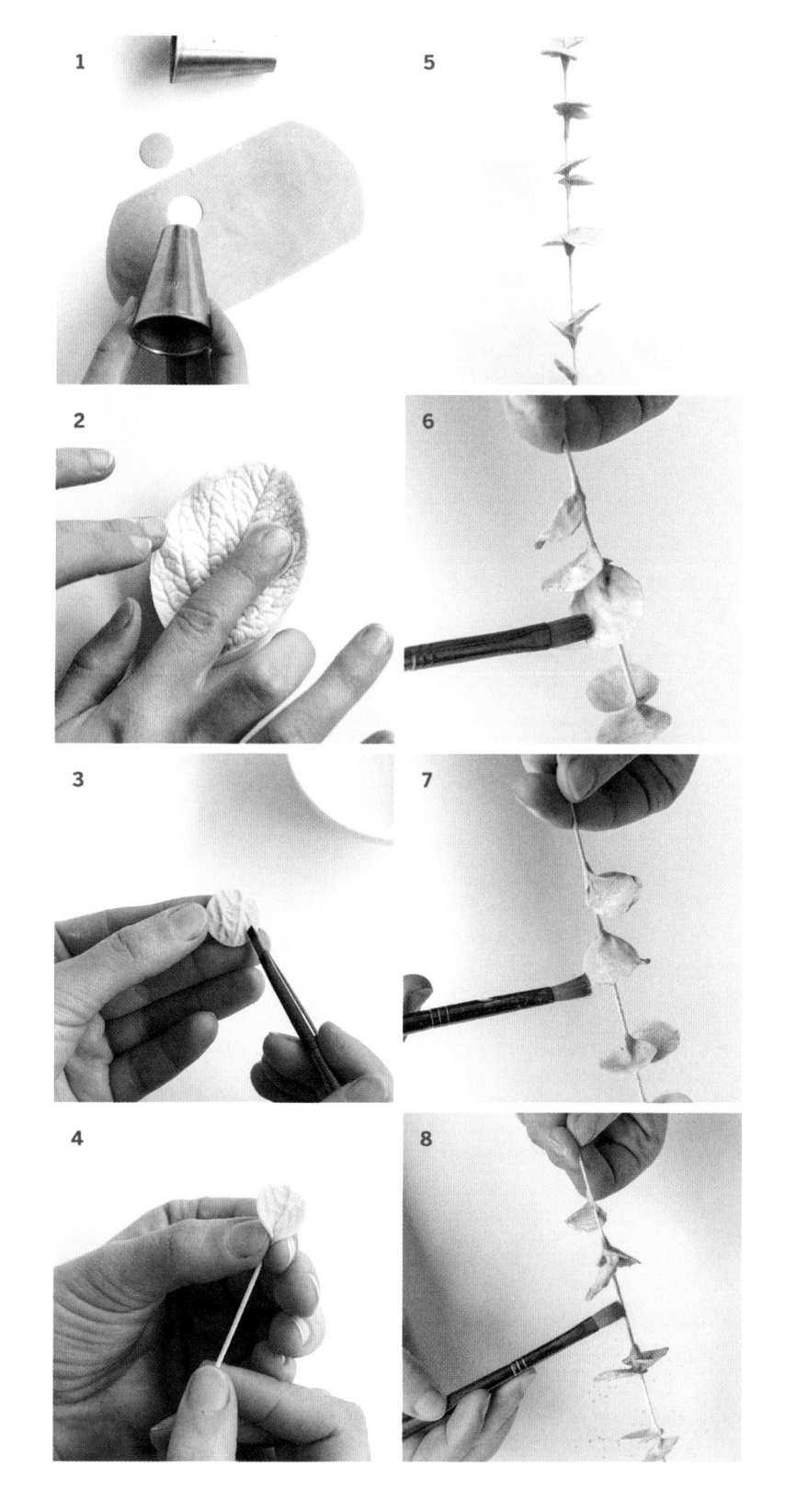

ARRANGING

FLOWERS

FOR SOME PEOPLE, this is the most mysterious and intimidating part of the flower-making process. Before you begin, be sure you've applied color to the back and sides of your pieces, not just on the front. Leaves can be particularly beautiful with their backs facing out. You don't want to limit your options simply because you forgot to color something.

When you're ready to arrange your flowers, have plenty of floral wire, pieces of floral tape already cut and stretched, and wire cutters all within arm's reach, as well as a palette of green and brown petal dusts to brush color on the stems. Take your time, relax, and make peace with the fact that there will be breakage. If the sound of a shattering petal or calyx is going to be upsetting, put on some music.

Have a game plan for what flowers and leaves you'd like to use, but be flexible when it comes to the exact placement. The flowers will dictate where they want to go based on their shapes. Unlike real flowers, which yield to pressure and create their own cushion, sugar flowers are inflexible and will crunch if you push or squeeze them. I'm just beginning to experiment with adding freshly made outer petals just before assembly to add some softness, but so far I've only tried this with larger, multilayered flowers.

It's very overwhelming to see all the individual components at once. You know just how long it took to make each one and how easy it would be to drop one (or more) of them! For that reason, I never try to gather everything into a bouquet at once.

Instead, without giving it a lot of thought, I start by taping a few things together and setting them aside. I refer to these as "packets." A packet can comprise whatever you like: two hydrangea blossoms and three leaves; one rose, an orchid, and a stem of baby eucalyptus—it's your choice. Instead of trying to create a uniform bouquet, height variation is key here. Hold the stems firmly together and wrap them with floral tape, starting at the top and wrapping the tape at a slight angle.

I continue in this way until I have perhaps ten packets rather than forty individual leaves and flowers. I then see which packets would be a good fit with each other. Sometimes I bring together four at a time, sometimes just two. Either way brings me closer to a full arrangement.

It's rare that everything ends up in the finished piece. For the most versatility in the final design, I prefer having the option of one or two larger arrangements, one small, and a couple additional packets. Perhaps they all end up on the cake, with a smaller arrangement on a lower tier and a packet on the edge of the cake stand. Or maybe the packet doesn't make the cut and I get to take it back to the studio and plant it in my Styrofoam "garden."

There is a method by which I assemble the components of a packet.

This little cluster of hydrangea, shown on the opposite page, is a good place to start. We're looking at the back of the arrangement. You'll see that the faces of the flowers are pointing out, up, and sideways, but not backward. Nothing needs

to be back there. A round arrangement placed between two tiers will either poke into the tier behind it, or have to be placed so close to the tier's edge that it is at risk of tearing through the cake. The flatter the back side of the arrangement, the better.

An arrangement that lives on the top tier needs to look beautiful from all angles. I still use packets with flat backs, but simply place the packets back to back so the flowers face outward. This way they don't crunch when I place them very close together.

You'll also see that not all the hydrangea blossoms are the same height. When I tape flowers together, I try to think of creating vertical interest. This not only helps keep the back of the arrangement flat, but also allows me to move things around within the arrangement without un-taping. If the top hydrangea blossom with the longest amount of exposed stem wants to be at the bottom instead of the top, I simply swing it around by manipulating the wire. It can live pretty much anywhere within that little packet.

Don't try to fight your flowers; work with their angles. I chose these four particular hydrangea blossoms because after rotating each, I found a way to nest them all together safely. Other blossoms didn't make the cut for this little packet, but they'll work for something else.

Even a broken blossom can find a home, with three intact petals showing and the missing one presumed to be hidden beneath another flower. Completely open, completely symmetrical flowers don't really like to be close to each other. A half-closed hydrangea or a leaf at an angle fills the gap between two ranunculi. A garden rose that somehow ended up a bit lopsided with too many petals off to one side is much easier to place than one that is perfectly round. An orchid with independently wired petals is fantastic in an arrangement; those petals and sepals can move anywhere you need them to.

Consider the foreground and the background of your arrangement, too. The lopsided garden rose can accommodate a taped spray of lamb's ear that extends slightly in front of the less bountiful side.

My idea of a "branch" is a strong central piece, often a couple of floral wires taped together, with leaves and/or flowers attached. It gives height, drama, movement, strength, and ease of insertion all in one. When I was constructing a large vase full of sugar flowers to be displayed in the White House, I learned very quickly that branches were the way to go. I built nearly everything on a branch, whether they grew that way in real life or not! That's the beauty of artistic license. A branch in an arrangement can be easily moved wherever you'd like. As a very straightforward example, see how I make a branch of little green leaves on page 287. Because the leaves are so light, a single 20-gauge wire is sufficient support.

As I'm demonstrating with the packet of roses and leaves shown on page 286, you'll need to return with a bit of petal dust to brush over the white tape.

For heavy flowers on a branch, use two 18-gauge wires. Tape the wires together from top to bottom before adding flowers or leaves.

A heavy-duty wire can also be added anytime you need a bit more length and strength in your "stem." The longer and stronger the stem, the more secure the arrangement will be within your cake tier. Clip the wire so it is the same length as the height of your tier.

ASSEMBLING A BRANCH

1 Align the end of the full-length wire so it is just slightly below the base of the leaf, leaving a tiny bit of the leaf's wire exposed.

2 Wrap tightly with floral tape and add another leaf.

3 Wrap and add another leaf. Continue down the wire, wrapping the tape at a slight angle and adding more leaves as you go.

INSERTING
FLOWERS
INTO A CAKE

POLY-DOWELS ARE LIKE EXTRA-STRONG STRAWS that come in different diameters. Think of a Poly-Dowel as a vase: It provides support for your arrangement and a clean environment for your stem. When you (or the catering staff) remove your sugar flowers before slicing into the cake, there is no messy buttercream or other cake fillings to clean off. The flowers can then be boxed in tissue paper and gifted to the client. For one or two small blossoms, a Poly-Dowel is not always necessary or practical. There's very little risk of them tearing through a tier, as long as they are lightweight. Just be sure that before inserting, you add a fresh piece of floral tape to cover any exposed wire at the base of the stem.

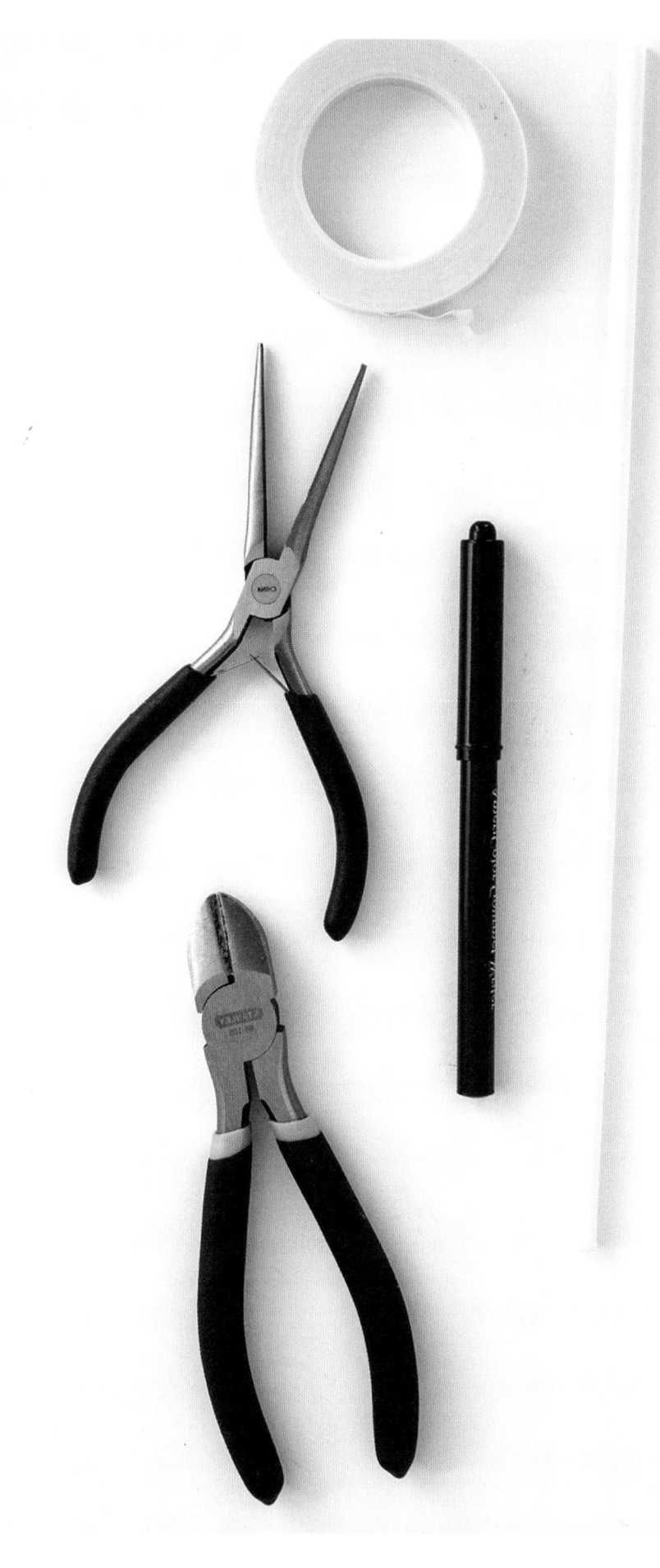

- Poly-Dowels (½ inch, ¼ inch)
- AmeriColor Gourmet Writer edible marker (black)
- Wire cutters
- White floral tape
- Needle-nose/jewelry pliers

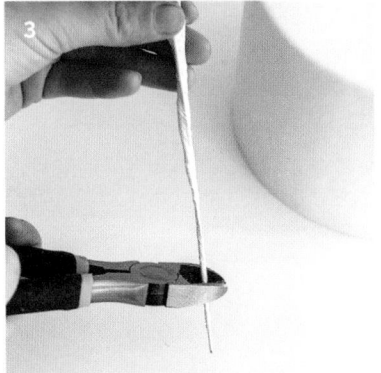

1   Identify which diameter Poly-Dowel is going to be appropriate for your arrangement. Be sure your cake is cold and firm. Take a measurement to determine the length for your Poly-Dowel. The bottom should go all the way down to the cake board and the top should rest just below the surface of the cake. Insert the dowel into the cake. Use edible marker to mark the Poly-Dowel where it meets the top of the cake. Remove the dowel, cut just below the mark, and reinsert the shortened dowel.

2   Place your arrangement next to the cake to get an idea of where it will sit.

3   Trim the stem as necessary.

4   Apply a fresh piece of floral tape that wraps all the way down and covers the exposed tip of the cut wire and back up the stem slightly. Always follow this step before inserting any wire into a cake. Place the arrangement into the dowel as far as you can, until you feel like your fingers are getting in the way or you feel resistance from the thicker part of the taped wire.

5   Use the needle-nose pliers to grip the stem near where it enters the cake and push down gently to secure it within the dowel.

6   Once the flowers are in the cake, you can adjust the individual components as needed.

ABOUT THE AUTHOR

MAGGIE AUSTIN IS A world-renowned cake designer whose trend-setting designs are redefining edible art. Drawing inspiration from her first career as a classical ballet dancer, Maggie creates designs that display graceful symmetry and an intense attention to detail along with a playful approach to tradition. She completed the prestigious L'Art de la Pâtisserie program at the French Pastry School with honors, studying under acclaimed pastry chefs Sébastien Canonne and Jacquy Pfeiffer. Together with her sister, Jessica, she brought her unique artistic vision to life when she launched Maggie Austin Cake in 2010 and has since reached a worldwide audience through extensive editorial media coverage including newspapers, magazines, blogs, and television. In her Alexandria, Virginia, studio, Maggie creates custom cakes and teaches decoration and sugar flowers to students all over the globe. Her work has been displayed at the White House and her exclusive clients include celebrities, royalty, her loving husband, Rob, and her dog, Bessie (who is partial to pear cake crumbs).

VISUAL INDEX

OMBRÉ FRILLS 63

DAHLIA FRILL 72

MOTTLED FRILLS 76

YELLOW ROSETTES 80

RIBBON-WRAPPED WATERCOLOR 82

JEWEL-TONED BLOSSOMS 89

ICELANDIC POPPIES &
FALLING PETALS 96

PETITE PINK BLOSSOMS 100

VINTAGE ENAMELED FLORAL
APPLIQUÉ 102

PANSY COOKIES 106

FLORAL EMBROIDERY 113

DAISY CAKES 120

TILE COOKIES 124

GOLD-LEAF WITH LACE OVERLAY 126

FRIDA 130

PEARLS & RIBBONS 136

FOLK ART BEADING 146

OYSTERS & PEARLS 150

ASYMMETRICAL PEARLS 152

CAMEO BAUBLES 156

ALABASTER BAS-RELIEF 161

STONE & HYDRANGEA 168

ELEPHANT CARAVAN 172

EMERALD TILES 176

FLORAL URNS 183

STAINED GLASS 187

SQUARE WATERCOLOR 194

ABSTRACT "PAINTING" 196

TEA TIN CAKES 198

IMPRESSIONIST COOKIES 200

PAINTED PETALS 207

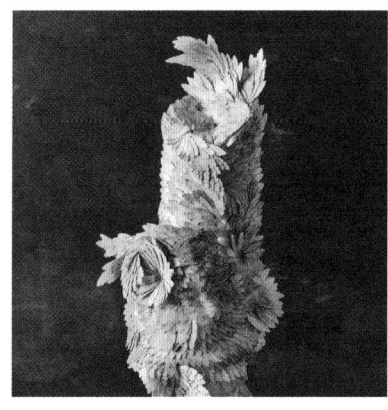

FEATHERS IN MOTION 214

FLOWER PETAL CASCADE 218

PURPLE OMBRÉ MINI CAKES 220

BUTTERFLY GARDEN 222

INDEX

NOTE: PAGE REFERENCES IN *italics* INDICATE PHOTOGRAPHS.